RESEARCH METHODS

Third Edition

Patrick McNeill and Steve Chapman

Routledge
Taylor & Francis Group

LONDON AND NEW YORK

First published 1985
by Tavistock Publications Ltd
Reprinted 1986, 1988

Reprinted 1989
by Routledge
2 Park Square, Milton Park, Abingdon, Oxon OX14 4RN

Simultaneously published in the USA and Canada
by Routledge
270 Madison Ave, New York, NY 10016

Second edition published 1990

Third edition published in 2005

Reprinted 2006

Routledge is an imprint of the Taylor & Francis Group, an informa business

© 1985, 1990 Patrick McNeill, 2005 Patrick McNeill and
Steve Chapman

Typeset in Plantin by
Keystroke, Jacaranda Lodge, Wolverhampton
Printed and bound in Great Britain by
TJ International Ltd, Padstow, Cornwall

British Library Cataloguing in Publication Data
A catalogue record for this book is available from the British Library

Library of Congress Cataloging in Publication Data
A catalog record for this book has been requested

ISBN 10: 0–415–34075–6 (hbk)
ISBN 10: 0–415–34076–4 (pbk)
ISBN 13: 978–0–415–34075–5 (hbk)
ISBN 13: 978–0–415–34076–2 (pbk)

Contents

Preface to First Edition

Good social science, like all science, is based on good evidence. That is why research methods are important. I hope that this book will help you to distinguish between good evidence and poor evidence, in sociology and in everyday life.

I have included a very large number of references to published studies. Some students may find this a bit daunting, but I would stress that you are not expected to read more than one or two yourself. It has taken me twenty years to have read this many, and you have not got that long. The reason for mentioning so many is that it helps you decide which ones look interesting, and also gives you a sporting chance of actually getting hold of a copy of at least one.

There are suggestions for study activities scattered throughout the book. They can be carried out either individually or in pairs or groups. Group work is often more valuable than individual work, and always more fun.

Lastly, I wish to thank the staff of St Albans College library, especially Joyce Omasta, for their help over the years. They provide a university-standard library service on FE college resources.

Patrick McNeill

Preface to Second Edition

I have made a number of changes for this revised edition, some prompted by the weaknesses of the first edition and others by changes in the way that A-level sociology is taught and examined.

In response to comments, I have broken up chapter 5 ('Other research methods') and relocated the sections at more appropriate points in the rest of the book.

I have included nearly fifty new references, some of which would have been in the first edition if there had been room and/or if I had known of their existence, and others of which have appeared in the last five years. I have, however, adhered to a guiding principle of the first edition, i.e. referring wherever possible to texts which students can reasonably expect to get hold of, rather than to texts which will impress teachers as to my knowledge of obscure studies.

Many have also been chosen in the hope that they will stimulate students to replicate or adapt them for their own research. Coursework projects, once an optional extra at A-level, are rapidly becoming *de rigueur* as an element in assessment schemes. This book is a discussion of research methods rather than an instruction manual, but I have altered the emphasis here and there and made other modifications to take account of this change, particularly in the discussions of the ethics of research. While I am a strong supporter of students doing their own research, I have reservations as to whether they are always properly briefed as to this aspect of their work. Tutors, at least, should look at Barnes (1975) and Bulmer (1982).

For those looking for a 'how-to-do-it' book to accompany this one, look at the references cited at the end of chapter 2. Incidentally, despite what at least one reviewer has said, Gomm and McNeill (1982), which is often referred to in the Activities sections of this book, is not out of print. For a stimulating discussion of the same range of topics as is covered in this book, see Shipman (1988).

Thanks again to the librarians at St Albans College, and also to Martin Bulmer for the conversation which guided part of pp. 7–8. Thanks too to Sharon Witherspoon, Steve Taylor, Geoff Payne, Peter Woods, Pat Mayhew, and Eileen Barker for the discussions which formed the basis of articles printed in *New Society* and in *New Statesman and Society*. Much of the material which had to be cut from those articles has informed the revision of this book.

Patrick McNeill

Preface to Third Edition

In the preface to the first edition of this book, published in 1985, I wrote 'Good social science, like all science, is based on good evidence. That is why research methods are important. I hope that this book will help you to distinguish between good evidence and poor evidence, in sociology and in everyday life.'

Twenty years on, all that remains true. The basic principles of what counts as good social science are unchanged. However, research methods have been developed and refined, more sources and types of evidence have become available, and far more research is being done. This third edition is intended to bring the book up to date not only by taking account of these developments but also by making reference to a wide range of research published in the fifteen years since the second edition was published.

I would like to take this opportunity to thank Steve Chapman very sincerely for the enormous amount of work he has put in to producing this edition of the book. It is Steve who has done the updating; I have only reviewed and commented on his work, a task which has been completely rewarding as he has kept faith with the aims and style of the original. I wish I could have done it as well as he has.

Patrick McNeill

When I first started out teaching sociology twenty years ago, Pat McNeill was a constant source of support. I didn't know the man but his books *The Handbook for Sociology Teachers* and *Research Methods* were absolutely crucial in terms of my survival in the classroom. In particular, *Research Methods* has seen literally hundreds of my students successfully through their A-level coursework. It has therefore been a privilege to have been invited to work with Pat on this new edition, and I can only hope that my contribution lives up to the very high standard he has set in terms of clearly and simply setting out the key methodological concepts, research tools and debates.

Steve Chapman

1

Research methods in sociology

'What is sociology about?' is probably the question that sociologists are asked more often than any other. A reasonable reply might be that sociologists are interested in those aspects of human behaviour which are the result of the social context in which we live. They do not concentrate on features which are the result of our physical or biological makeup. Sociology stresses the patterns and the regularities of social life which are, most of the time, orderly and largely predictable.

The next question is then, typically, 'But what do you actually do?' and it is to this question that this book is addressed. While there is, as you may know, considerable variation and disagreement among sociologists, they are united in the conviction that argument that is based on sound evidence is superior to argument based on false evidence, limited evidence, or no evidence. Evidence has to be collected from the social world around us, and this requires empirical research to be done. 'Empirical', in this context, simply means 'based on evidence from the real world' in contrast to 'theoretical', which refers to ideas that are abstract or purely analytical. Theories must be tested against the real world, 'Theory, in fact, is the building which is made from the hard-won bricks of research studies' (Mann 1985). This still leaves open the question of what counts as sound evidence, and this in turn leads to a central theme of this book: 'How can we collect sound evidence about the social world that can be used to increase our understanding of that world?'

Over the years, sociologists have used a wide variety of methods of data collection and analysis. They have studied an even wider variety of aspects of social life, from such matters as how people avoid bumping into each other in the street to topics as wide-ranging as the causes of the rise of capitalism. In fact, a brief history of sociology since the end of the last century is an effective way of introducing the variety of research styles and some of the topics studied.

The late nineteenth century

Modern sociology is usually thought to have its roots in the work of classical sociologists who worked at the end of the nineteenth and the beginning of the twentieth century. These writers, of whom Marx (1818–83), Weber (1864–1920) and Durkheim (1858–1917) are usually regarded as the most important, were essentially theorists, who based their analysis of what was happening to the rapidly changing European societies of that time on evidence from historians and other sources rather than on their own original research.

At about the same time, i.e. the end of the nineteenth century, Charles Booth (1840–1916) was conducting one of the first major social surveys, which he published between 1891 and 1903 in seventeen volumes entitled *Life and Labour of the People in London*. Booth, prompted by a number of newspaper and magazine articles, was concerned to find out the true extent of poverty among the working classes of London at that time, and he collected vast quantities of data about them, using a combination of early survey techniques and other less statistical methods. He went from house to house in certain areas of the East End of London, painstakingly recording the number of residents, the number of rooms they occupied, their living conditions, their income, diet, clothing and so on. He also collected their own accounts of the experience of poverty and their feelings about it. He spent some time actually living as a boarder in houses in the areas that he was studying and making detailed studies of particular families.

Anthropology and the Chicago School

The first third of the twentieth century saw the development of anthropological fieldwork. Researchers who were interested in the way of life of what were regarded as primitive peoples went to live among them to study their societies from the inside. Previously, investigations like this had been done mainly from the outsider's point of view, and it was men like Evans-Pritchard (1902–73), Radcliffe-Brown (1881–1955) and, particularly, Malinowski (1884–1942), who determined that the only really effective way of understanding the way of life of these peoples was to go and live among them for an extended period of time, learning their language and becoming accepted as a member of their social groups.

Another very important school of sociological research developed under the influence of Robert E. Park (1864–1944) at the University of Chicago in the period between the two world wars. They based almost all their work on anthropological techniques, but they were interested in the wide variety of lifestyles that they found on their own doorsteps in Chicago, rather than in simple tribal societies. They used a method that became known as 'participant observation', in which the researcher both observes the social processes of a group and actually participates in the life of that group. They combined this with interviewing, some taking of life-histories and the use of various official records and other documents.

In this way, these researchers built up a picture of lifestyles in Chicago at that time, especially those of certain deviant groups such as hoboes and gang-members.

Postwar research

After the Second World War, there was a change of emphasis among sociologists concerning what research techniques produced the best data. Under the influence of researchers in America such as Paul Lazarsfeld (1901–70), greater emphasis was put on the need for proof and on the importance of data being as objective as possible, i.e. that it should be free of any influence of the individual researcher who happened to collect it. It was argued that, using the right data-collection techniques, it should be possible to assemble information about the social world that is free of bias, and that could be analysed using the statistical techniques which had been developed. The emphasis in this work was on the collection of statistical data, i.e. in the form of numbers, rather than descriptions of particular ways of life. The intention was to uncover the causes of human social behaviour, often with a view to influencing social policy in order to reduce social problems and generally improve the quality of life. This approach was strongly influenced by the methods of natural science and is known as positivism. The emphasis during the 1950s was on surveys but these were often supplemented with other methods.

During the 1960s, there were great changes in sociology in Britain. There was a reaction against the kind of sociology that encouraged the survey style of social research, and a move towards participant observation and other fieldwork techniques, such as informal or 'unstructured' interviews. Some sociologists, strongly influenced by American sources, became converted to ethnomethodology, which set out completely to recast the objectives of sociological enquiry (see pp. 128–30).

For several years, in the late 1960s and the early 1970s, sociologists seemed to spend as much time and effort arguing about how they should be thinking about and studying the social world as they did in actually doing research. These disputes were once over-dramatically described as 'British sociology's wars of religion', and, while sociology emerged in the late 1970s as a stronger discipline than it had been previously, this was not a period which was very productive in terms of sociology's public image. However, some excellent studies were done at this time, many using fieldwork techniques and participant observation rather than surveys.

There were important developments in social research in the 1980s, one of which was the growth of feminist research (Roberts 1981). Feminist scholars have shown how all academic disciplines have been dominated by a male view of the world. In social science, this has meant that women have been virtually ignored, except as they related to men, and that the male has been seen as the norm. Studies of social mobility, of schools, of work, of leisure, of youth culture, even of the family, either ignored women or saw them only through male eyes. Feminist research has begun to restore the balance by researching women's lives, by demonstrating how far British society is dominated by men and by reinterpreting evidence originally produced by men. The purpose of feminist enquiry is to bring about female emancipation and to devise more open and equal methodological techniques suited to researching women, their issues and views of the world.

The 1980s also saw the emergence of the structuration theory of Anthony Giddens. He aimed to show how aspects of the social structure of society, particularly social class, ethnicity and gender, interact with the social meanings held by social actors, to bring about or constrain social action. Giddens recognized that people's actions are the result of their interpretations of their social reality but he points out that people's choice of action is often limited by structural factors which are largely beyond their control. For example, we have seen in recent years, major changes in female aspirations in regard to education. Young females now interpret further and higher qualifications as a necessary step to establishing a good career. However, the choices that result may be constrained by the patriarchal structure of work which has traditionally suited male working patterns. Giddens's theory strongly encouraged the use of multiple methods. Quantitative methods were seen as suited to exploring the influence of the social structure whilst qualitative methods aimed to uncover how people interpreted that social structure. Taylor's (1982) research into suicide on the London Underground is a good example of a piece of research influenced by Giddens in terms of both theory and practice.

The 1990s saw the emergence of a postmodernist critique of research practice. This critique suggests that 'truth' and 'authenticity' are unattainable goals for researchers because postmodernists claim that these do not exist as universal and objective realities. Rather, they are concepts relative to time and place. There is therefore no objective standard to judge that one version of the 'truth' is better than another. Postmodernists reject the 'expert' status of the sociological researcher because the researcher is only one interpreter of reality. The researcher's claim to 'truth' is no more valuable than anyone else's. Postmodernists also reject the concept of 'validity' which they see as an attempt to impose a set of rules in regard to how research should be conducted.

Postmodernist observations of research have not escaped criticism themselves. Devine and Heath note that postmodernism's 'wholesale dismissal of conventional criteria for assessing social research can easily collapse into a rather hopeless relativism and consequently an ability to contribute to public debate' (1999: 210). Gomm is even more dismissive when he notes that there is no place for a theory that denies the existence of truth in a book on research methods.

In the last decade, there has been an outbreak of peace in sociology's own particular conflicts. In research terms, this has shown itself in the way that it has become perfectly acceptable to use a wide variety of research techniques in one study, and to use different techniques for the study of different topics. This may seem blindingly obvious to the newcomer to the discipline, but there were very good reasons for the disputes that took place. The arguments that are now available to justify the use of particular methods are much more convincing than they used to be. At the same time, it should not be forgotten that some writers had been advocating the use of multiple methods for years.

More use is also being made of secondary data, such as personal documents, official statistics, and the huge collection of data held in the UK Data Archive at Essex University (www.data-archive.ac.uk). There have been rapid developments in techniques for the storage, manipulation and retrieval of data, using new technology. Historical sociology is also expanding, with sociologists paying more attention to history and with historians becoming more sociological.

What is research for?

Having started this chapter with two questions, we can now add two more. What is sociological research for? Why is it done at all?

Sociological research, like all scientific enquiry is fundamentally prompted by simple human curiosity, an indispensable quality if research is to be both successful and enjoyable. But curiosity can take different forms.

Descriptive research and explanatory research

Some research aims only to describe, in detail, a situation or set of circumstances. It aims to answer questions like 'how many?' and 'who?' and 'what is happening?' The writer wishes to do no more than add to our knowledge of the social world, simply for the sake of knowing. Other research sets out to explain a social phenomenon. It asks 'why?' and tries to find the answer to a problem. This may be a social problem or a sociological problem.

Social problems are those aspects of social life that cause private unhappiness or public friction, and are identified by those in power as needing some kind of social policy to deal with them. 'Social policy' refers to those actions of governments that have a direct effect on the welfare of the citizens of a country. This may mean providing income for certain groups of people, as through the British social security system. It may mean providing services, such as education or a health service, which are available to all, or the home help service, which is available to those judged to be most in need of it. Sociological research can provide government with the information needed to identify the size of a problem, and to plan a response to that problem. This does not mean that governments always take action when researchers identify a social problem, or act upon their findings. They are free to ignore social research, and often do.

A sociological problem is any aspect of social life that needs explaining. It may also be a social problem, but sociologists are just as interested in trying to explain 'normal' behaviour and events as they are in trying to explain the deviant or the abnormal. Much research is concerned only with increasing our knowledge of how societies work, and explaining patterns of social behaviour. It may have implications for social policy, but this is not the prime purpose.

The distinction between descriptive research and explanatory research is often very blurred. Any explanation requires description, and it is difficult, or perhaps impossible, to describe something without at the same time explaining it.

Action research

In recent years, action research has become much more widely used, especially in research into education and schooling. Action research takes the form of a systematic enquiry, often conducted by practitioners and researchers working together, which is designed to yield practical results. These results are then used to improve a specific aspect of practice (e.g. teaching and learning). Like all social science research, the results are made public so that other people can check and test them.

Whatever, the reason for research, it must be remembered that the basic value, as in all science, is truth.

Three important concepts

Three key concepts are used throughout this book. Their meanings will become clear with use, but it is sensible to introduce them briefly at this stage.

Reliability

If a method of collecting evidence is reliable, it means that anybody else using this method, or the same person using it at another time, would come up with the same results. The research could be repeated, and the same results would be obtained. For example, an experiment in a chemistry lesson should always 'work'. It should always produce the result that is expected, whoever is doing it, at whatever time, provided that the proper procedures are followed.

Some methods in sociology are regarded as being more reliable than others. Any method that involves a lone researcher in a situation that cannot be repeated, like much participant observation research, is always in danger of being thought unreliable.

Validity

Validity refers to the problem of whether the data collected is a true picture of what is being studied. Is it really evidence of what it claims to be evidence of? The problem arises particularly when the data collected seems to be a product of the research method used rather than of what is being studied.

Suppose we were making an enquiry into people's leisure habits. If we designed a questionnaire to ask people what they did in their free time, how would we know whether the answers we received gave us a true picture of how they spend that time; or a picture of what they will say to a researcher when they are asked the question? This is not just a matter of people telling lies. They may genuinely believe what they are saying, but actual observation of what they do might well produce a different picture. This is particularly relevant in attitude surveys, where it is important not to assume that people's expressed attitudes, on, say, race relations, are consistent with their actual behaviour.

This is always a nagging doubt about any survey-style research. It must be accepted that what we are collecting is people's answers to questions, which is not necessarily a true picture of their activities. In laboratory experiments, we may be getting a picture of how people behave in laboratories, but can we be sure that this is how they behave in the real world (see Chapter 3).

Representativeness

This refers to the question of whether the group of people or the situation that we are studying are typical of others. If they are, then we can safely conclude that what is true of this group is also true of others. We can generalize from the example that we have studied. If we do not know whether they are representative, then we cannot claim that our conclusions have any relevance to anybody else at all. As we shall see in Chapter 2, careful sampling methods have been devised to try to ensure representativeness in survey research, but many other methods do not involve systematic sampling, and there must always be a question as to the representativeness of their findings and conclusions.

Choice of research topic

This is affected by many things, most of which are to do with the interests and the values of the researcher, which are usually interrelated. Peter Townsend has had a life-long commitment to the needs of the poor and the powerless, and his studies of the elderly (1957) and the poor (1979) are the result of that commitment. Researchers will also be influenced by current debates in the academic world. Thus Goldthorpe and Lockwood (Goldthorpe *et al.* 1969) carried out their research among the manual workers of Luton at a time when academic opinion was saying that such people were beginning to take on middle-class characteristics. Their research questioned this but the idea emerged again in the mid-1980s and inspired further research by Marshall *et al.* (1988) and Devine (1992). The commitment of sociologists such as Mirza (1992) and Sewell (1997) to studying the educational experience of young African-Caribbean girls and boys has been derived to some extent from their own background as African-Caribbeans whilst Ken Plummer's research has pioneered research into sexual identity and especially lesbian, gay and bisexual lives.

Choice of topic will also be affected by the funding of the research. Researchers who depend on grants from organizations like the Economic and Social Research Council, or from private foundations like the Gulbenkian, Ford, or Joseph Rowntree, will only be able to carry out their enquiry if it is approved by the organization in question. Academic researchers working in higher education have to convince the relevant committees in their institution that the work is important enough for scarce resources to be devoted to it. Sometimes research is commissioned, and the researcher is approached by government, a local authority, a business, or a charitable organization to carry out a specific enquiry on their behalf. This will almost invariably be linked to the policy objectives of the sponsoring organization. Broadly speaking, it is easier to obtain funding for explanatory research that seems to provide guidance to policy-makers than for purely academic research, and for research that is statistically based than for research that is more qualitative in its approach. The choice of research topic is not made in a vacuum, but is influenced both by the researcher and by the context in which the research is to be done.

This does not automatically mean that the research is biased. Just because researchers have strong feelings about what they are investigating, it does not automatically follow that their findings will be slanted in favour of their own beliefs and values. Indeed, this is a major difference between social science and journalism. The social scientist must conduct a fair and balanced enquiry, not allowing personal or political values to affect what is discovered and reported. Values will influence the choice of topic, as they do in all branches of science, but methods should be value-free.

It is also worth remembering that choice of topic is affected by the power of the subjects of the research to resist the investigation. How far such resistance is possible varies according to the research methods employed but, generally speaking, we know more about the poor and the powerless than we do about the rich and the powerful.

Ethics

Research can have a very powerful impact on people's lives. The researcher must always think very carefully about the impact of the research and how he/she ought to behave, so that no harm comes to the subject of the research or to society in general. In other words, ethics or moral principles must guide research. There is a growing awareness that the people on whom sociologists conduct their research have rights and that researchers have responsibilities and obligations to their research subjects. Generally, it has been agreed by British sociologists that there are six broad ethical rules that should underpin all sociological research.

First, many researchers believe that all research participants have a right to know what the research is about and to refuse to take part in it or to answer particular questions. This is informed consent – people should know research is being carried out upon them and how the results will be used so that they can make an intelligent choice as to whether they want to take part. However, informed consent is not always a straightforward matter. For example, very young children or people with learning disabilities may not be able to fully understand what the researcher is doing.

Second, it is argued that sociologists should not engage in deception. Information must not be kept from those taking part in the research and researchers must not lie about the purpose of the research. Subjects should be aware at all times that they are participating in a research study. It is argued that it is particularly deceptive to establish friendships in order to manipulate data from them. This is particularly problematic when the data gained by the sociologist involves very personal and sensitive information that would not have been passed on through interviews or questionnaires. Oakley was very aware that the first-time mothers who featured in her research *From Here to Maternity* may have been cynical about her sociological role because they lost their 'friend' and 'confidante' when the research ended. However, as we shall see later, not all sociologists accept these propositions. Some argue that deceit can produce data that cannot be produced under more honest circumstances, and the value of such data to policy-makers justifies the ethical costs.

Third, most sociologists agree that the privacy of research subjects should be safeguarded as much as possible. However, sociological research is by its very nature intrusive – sociologists are generally interested in what goes on in families, how people behave, what they think, etc., and consequently, this can be a difficult ethical objective to achieve.

Fourth, the problem of maintaining privacy can be countered by keeping the identity of research participants secret. Confidentiality means that the information an individual gives to the researcher cannot be traced back to that individual. Ethical researchers are careful to disguise the identity of individual participants when they write up their research. If people know they cannot be identified, they may be more willing to reveal all sorts of personal and private matters. In other words, confidentiality and anonymity may increase the validity of the data collected.

Fifth, most sociologists would agree that research participants should be protected from any sort of physical harm. This is seldom a problem. One of the reasons that sociologists rarely use experiments, for example, is that these may lead to the subjects being harmed by the experiment. However, some sociological research may harm someone emotionally, for example, if they are asked insensitive questions. Surveys of crime victims, for example, may trigger memories people would prefer to forget or create fear of crime. There may also be harmful social consequences of sociological research. For example, people's reputations can be damaged by published research. They may feel that they have been misrepresented and exposed to ridicule. There is also a danger that people may face punishment or controls because of something a sociologist published.

Finally, sociological researchers need to think about legality and immorality, especially those that are involved in covert forms of research. In particular, sociologists need to avoid being drawn into situations where they may commit crimes or possibly help in or witness deviant acts. As we shall see later, especially when examining the method of observation, sociologists have not always successfully avoided this type of behaviour.

All the above ethical problems are important because quite simply if people do not trust sociologists, the validity of the data collected by the sociologists will not reflect what respondents are truly thinking or doing.

Choosing a research method

Anybody who wishes to study any aspect of the world about them has to decide what methods they are going to use. Their decision is made on the basis of their assumptions about what kind of thing it is they are studying. Scientists who study the natural world, including plants, minerals and animals, assume that the things they are studying are not aware of their own existence, and that the causes of their behaviour are outside their control. They do not choose to behave as they do. Accordingly, they can be studied on the assumption that everything there is to be known about them can be found through observation of their external behaviour.

Such assumptions cannot be taken for granted with the study of human subjects. As we saw earlier, when we briefly reviewed the history of sociological research, the period between the early 1960s and the early 1990s was characterized by a debate about how we should go about researching society between two schools of thought known as positivism and phenomenology.

Positivism

Positivism is a philosophical concept, and refers to a particular set of assumptions about the world and about appropriate ways of studying it. In general, positivists see 'society' as more important than the 'individual'. For example, they point out that individuals are born, take their place in society and then die, but society continues largely undisturbed. Moreover, positivists suggest that people are the puppets of society, i.e. they are controlled by social forces emanating from the organization of society. This is because they believe that just as there are natural laws governing the behaviour of chemicals, elements, plants, animals, etc., so there are social forces or laws governing and determining the operations of the social world, particularly our everyday experiences and life chances. Such laws are the product of the way a society or social group is socially organized, i.e. its social structure, and are beyond human influence.

Both functionalism and Marxism are positivist theories because they believe that individual behaviour is less important for our understanding of social life than the social structure of society. Functionalism stresses the need for individuals to be socialized into a value consensus which shapes and controls the behaviour of members of society, and brings about social order. It is consequently very difficult to resist social pressures to conform to certain values and norms such as achieving in education, working for a living, etc. Marxism is also positivist because it sees human behaviour as shaped or determined by the economic organization of capitalist society. Marxists argue that capitalist societies like the UK are characterized by profound class inequalities in wealth and income distribution, education, health, mortality, etc. In particular, Marxists argue that our behaviour is a product of our socio-economic positions within capitalist society. In other words, the social class to which we belong exerts a strong influence on our life-chances and outcomes, e.g. whether or not we live to a ripe old age, what causes our death, what standard of living we experience and so on.

Positivists see sociology as the 'science of society' and believe that the behaviour of human beings can be objectively and scientifically measured in much the same way as the subject matter of the natural sciences. They consequently argue that sociologists should adopt the logic and methods of the natural sciences in their exploration of how the social structure of society shapes people's behaviour and actions. This approach, they argue, will produce scientific laws of human behaviour. Predictions about the social world can be made, and this makes possible a certain amount of social engineering. This should lead to a reduction of poverty, or crime, or social unrest, or whatever it is that the writer believes is an undesirable aspect of human affairs. In other words, there is absolute truth and it can be used to create a better society.

If we examine positivist principles further, we can see certain assumptions about the characteristics that scientific method should ideally have. First, research should be objective or value-free. In other words, the sociologist should be neutral and not allow their personal or political opinions and prejudices to bias any aspect of their research method or their interpretation of the data they collect. The sociologist should be determined to pursue scientific truths with an open mind. One way in which to ensure objectivity is to carry out research under controlled conditions. Natural scientists have the advantage of conducting experiments in laboratories. However, sociologists very rarely use laboratory experiments and have had to devise alternative methods of control. As we shall see, positivists have developed sampling techniques and rules of questionnaire design, as well as keeping at a distance from the people whom they are studying, in order to maintain what they regard as objective control.

Second, positivists regard reliability as the most important characteristic of scientific method. They argue that the sociological research method used in any piece of research should be able to be repeated by other sociologists in order to verify and check its scientific accuracy. The research method should be open to inspection, criticism and testing by other researchers. Positivists, as we shall see, regard research methods that produce quantitative data as more reliable than other methods because they are normally organized in standardized and systematic ways, e.g. a logical sequence of set questions involving tick-boxes is easily replicated by another sociologist.

Third, the research should produce mainly quantitative or statistical data that can be converted into tabular or graphical information. As we shall see, some primary research methods, notably the survey questionnaire and the structured interview are most likely to produce this type of data. Some sociologists will also use secondary quantitative data in the form of official statistics. Such data can, then, be observed for patterns or trends which should result in the uncovering of correlations or links between aspects of social structure and social behaviour. Positivists argue that such correlations can help uncover cause and effect relationships which can establish 'social laws' about human behaviour, e.g. some positivists might go so far as to suggest that changes in the economy have 'caused' profound changes in the home in terms of the relationship between the spouses resulting in increases in the number of women petitioning for divorce.

The positivist approach to the study of the social world continued to be influential in sociology up to the 1960s. It was by no means the only approach, but it was the one that had the most status, and sociologists were anxious to establish their new discipline in the academic world. In this period, we therefore see the extensive use of quantitative methods such as the social survey which incorporates questionnaires and structured interviews. As we have seen, positivists tend to believe that the causes of human behaviour lie *outside* of the individual in the structural forces of society. Consequently, they tend to take a 'macro' approach to the study of society in that they are primarily concerned with examining the relationships between different parts of the social structure, e.g. the impact of the economy on education, rather than how individuals see the social world. They therefore see little point in employing qualitative research methods that attempt to see the world through the eyes of individuals such as participant observation and unstructured interviews.

Phenomenology and interpretive sociology

As already stated, Marx, Durkheim, and other classical sociologists were much influenced by positivist approaches to scientific study. However, another of the classical sociologists, Max Weber, had reservations about this approach.

Weber argued that there is an important difference between the subject matter of sociology and the subject matter of the natural sciences. This important difference is that people are active, conscious beings, aware of what is going on in a social situation, and capable of making choices about how to act. Natural phenomena have no meaning for those involved in them. What makes a social event social is that all those involved give it the same meaning. They all interpret what is happening in broadly the same way. If they do not, social interaction cannot take place. If we are to explain some event in the social world, our explanation has to take into account what the people involved feel and think about it. We must not regard them simply as helpless puppets.

Durkheim, of course, knew perfectly well that people have insight and understanding of what is going on around them, but his explanations of social phenomena did not stress this aspect of social life. Weber believed that it was not enough just to show the external causes. It was also necessary to show how these causes actually influenced people's thinking about the world. Thus, in his explanation of the growth of capitalism (see pp. 84–5), he showed not only that Calvinism was the independent variable that was only present in Europe, and thus was an important cause of the rise of capitalism, but he also went to great pains to spell out why it was that a belief in Calvinism would make someone behave in the way he described. The explanation is adequate at the level of meaning, just as much as at the level of cause.

This emphasis on meaning and consciousness is also a central feature of the sociology of the Chicago School, influenced as it was by the theories of George Mead, a philosopher at that university. Mead was especially interested in the concept of self, and delivered a series of lectures in the 1920s which were later published as *Mind, Self and Society*. In these lectures, Mead argued that a sense of self, of who one is in relation to others, can only develop in a social context. Children have to learn to 'take the attitude of the other', that is, they have to learn to see the social world as others see it. We all have to learn to put ourselves in other people's shoes (or, to put it more vividly, to get inside other people's heads), if we are to interact socially. The central feature of social life is that actions are the result of people's interpretations of the situation that they are in. People interpret the actions of others and react according to that interpretation. Most of the time, such interpretations are shared by all those involved and social life proceeds smoothly enough. There are, however, occasions when interpretations differ, and more or less serious social breakdown occurs. The causes of social action lie in people's 'definition of the situation', their interpretation of events, not in some pattern of objective laws that govern from outside.

It follows that, if we want to explain social actions, we have first to understand them in the way that the participants do. We must learn to see the world from their standpoint. Validity, i.e. seeing the world as it really is, is all-important. Interpretivists strongly believe that unique and trusting relationships should be established with those being studied so that a true picture of their lives is constructed. We must develop research methods that make it possible for us to do this. This is the tradition of social research that has given rise to ethnographic studies, particularly the technique of participant observation. Data collected in this way is qualitative in form rather than quantitative, that is, it concentrates on presenting the quality of the way of life described rather than on presenting statistics. Qualitative data is in the form of words rather than numbers. Much of the research report is composed of word-for-word quotation from those being studied.

These interpretive methods became even more popular with the emergence and growth of phenomenological sociology in the 1960s. Phenomenology, like positivism, is a philosophy in its own right which has been applied to the study of sociology. Edmund Husserl (1859–1938) founded phenomenology in the early part of the twentieth century, and Alfred Schutz (1899–1959) applied Husserl's ideas to the study of social life. Schutz's work, in turn, was brought to a wider audience by Berger and Luckmann in their book *The Social Construction of Reality* (1967). They argued that social reality is not out there, waiting to be experienced by social actors, even though it may often feel as though it is. Instead, we actively create (or construct) social reality through social interaction. It then takes on the appearance of existing independently of us, and is perceived as influencing our behaviour from outside. Berger and Luckmann discussed how social actors construct reality, and the way in which they then experience this reality as external to them. While much of their discussion is highly theoretical, it has given rise to research into how reality is constructed at an everyday level. This approach has led some sociologists into ethnomethodology, which will be described on pp. 128–30.

All these influences, taken together and separately, have led to the growth of those research methods that emphasize the importance of studying social life in its natural setting, and describing it as it is seen and experienced by those involved.

The emphasis of these methods is on the validity of the data collected, which may be achieved at the price of its reliability or its representativeness. Social reality is seen as 'intersubjective', i.e. it exists in the shared consciousness of actors. It is not objective or external, but is a construction of shared meanings and interpretations. Man is a conscious, active, purposeful social being, rather than being subject to external influences over which he has no control. The task of sociological research is to describe these shared meanings, which may, in turn, make it possible to explain why people behave as they do.

The range of methods

The debate between positivist and interpretivist sociology has often been presented in such a way as to imply that the gulf between them is deep and wide, and that they are as different as chalk and cheese. Pawson (1999) argues that this is both a simplification and an exaggeration. He suggests that the idea that these two approaches have nothing in common and are therefore irreconcilable is a methodological myth. Pawson points out that such myths are damaging because they may have convinced a generation of sociology students that there are 'heroes and villains' when it comes to choosing research methods. It is implied that 'no good sociologist should get his (or her) hands dirty with numbers' (p. 32) and therefore, the only authentic research methods are those that forge close, empathetic relationships with their subjects. However, Pawson makes three important observations about this false dichotomy. First, he argues that positivism and phenomenology are not polar opposites – they face identical problems and need to adopt common solutions. Second, he points out that a great deal of social enquiry has side-stepped the theory war and successfully employed 'a combination of qualitative and quantitative methods – apparently without the researcher suffering signs of schizophrenia' (p. 32). Third, he notes that today's methodological disputes are more likely to be 'family feuds', e.g. ethnographers arguing about how participant observation might be best organized in order to best reproduce social reality. It is therefore important not to think of positivist and interpretivist research styles as falling into two completely separate compartments. It is better to think of them as being on a scale, as shown in Figure 1.1.

On this scale, it is apparent that the more people who are studied, the less the researcher becomes personally involved with them. If the researcher thinks personal involvement is important, the price to be paid is that fewer people can be studied. Where the survey researcher may claim reliability and representativeness, the ethnographer will claim validity. The survey enthusiast will point out the dangers of bias and unreliability in ethnography, and stress how the representativeness of a sample can be calculated precisely. The ethnographer may concede all this, but would point out that it is not much use being able to produce the same results over and over again, and to say how representative they are, if they are invalid in the first place. The questionnaire may produce the same statistics whenever it is used, but this may be just a matter of repeating the same distortions. The survey style of research imposes a structure on that which is being researched, rather than allowing the structure to emerge from the data as it is collected. A survey can collect data only about those things which are included in the questionnaire, and this may omit crucial points. An ethnographic study, on the other hand, can never be repeated in exactly the same way, so there is no way of checking its findings.

Most researchers would now accept that it is sensible to use a mixture of methods. In fact, the multiple methods approach has been widespread in sociology for years. It has generally been used in two broad ways although the reasons for using each approach often overlap. First, methodological pluralism refers to the employment by the social researcher of more than one method of research in order to build up a fuller and more comprehensive picture of social life. For example, qualitative research might be used to produce extracts of

Figure 1.1 Methods of data collection

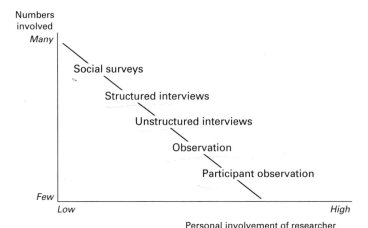

Source: Worsley 1977: 89.

verbatim conversation that gives life to the 'why' and 'how' of the patterns and trends revealed by the statistics produced by official reports or questionnaires. Phizacklea and Wolkowitz (1995) in their study on homeworking women used a national survey, in-depth interviewing and case studies in order to increase the validity of the picture they painted of this type of work.

Second, triangulation refers to the use of multiple methods to cross-check and verify the reliability of a particular research tool and the validity of the data collected. The term is borrowed from land surveying, and means simply that you get a better view of things by looking at them from more than one direction. Usually triangulation involves combining quantitative and qualitative methods in order to check on the accuracy of the data gathered by each method, i.e. observation data might be verified by using follow-up interviews with those being observed to confirm the validity of the researcher's observations or by asking respondents to keep detailed diaries documenting the motives for their behaviour. Questionnaire responses might be checked by carrying out unstructured interviews with key respondents. Qualitative research may also produce hypotheses which can be checked using quantitative methods. For example, observation may uncover unexpected behaviour that could be further investigated using a survey.

There are some disadvantages with these multiple methods approaches. They are often expensive and produce vast amounts of data which can be difficult to analyse. Bryman (1988) notes that in both triangulation and methodological pluralism, priority tends to be given to one method at the expense of the others, i.e. they are not accorded equal status. This is partly because as Devine and Heath (1999) note, experts in survey research are rarely equally proficient in ethnography and vice versa. They also point out that sometimes a combination of methods can actually throw up contradictory findings – this then leads to the problem of what to do with such data. Should it be discarded? Should the researcher attempt to reconcile the data? Despite these potential problems, however, there are few areas of social life where one research method alone is sufficient to gain a meaningful insight into people's lives, and consequently sociological research is becoming increasingly pluralistic.

Many of the studies listed on pp. 46 and 119 use multiple methods. In terms of theory, all this ties in with the recognition that, while people's actions are a result of their interpretation of a situation, their interpretations and their choices may also be limited by structural factors external to them and beyond their control.

Further reading

For examples of research designs involving a variety of techniques, try Barker (1984), Cohen (1987), Phizacklea and Wolkowitz (1995), Finch and Mason (1993) and Gregson and Lowe (1994).

Practical issues influencing choice of method

While the theoretical debates outlined above have great influence on the choice of research method, practical issues must not be forgotten. These are not wholly distinct from theory, but can be stated rather more briefly. The main ones are time, labour-power, money and choice of topic.

All social research takes time, but a study based on participant observation usually requires at least two years. In most such studies, the researcher or team of researchers spends between six months and two years 'in the field', and there is then a long period of analysing the data and writing the research report. There is no short cut possible in any of this. Writing up transcripts of interviews and identifying themes is just a lengthy business. Of course, in most such studies the researcher has begun to identify themes, classify and index the data while the research is still in progress, but there is always a great deal more to be done. Even then there will be another year to wait before a book is published.

Survey-based research is usually quicker to carry out. It is important not to rush it, but once the questionnaire or interview schedule has been finalized, data collection can proceed quite quickly and, if the questionnaire has been well designed, data analysis presents less of a problem since statistics can be processed with the help of a computer. The writing of the report still has to be done, but taken all in all, surveys can usually be completed in a shorter time than can ethnographic research. There are exceptions. Townsend's study *Poverty in the United Kingdom*, published in 1979, was based on research carried out in 1969. At the other extreme, the series on *British Social Attitudes* is published annually (Jowell *et al.*).

The size of the research team will have an important bearing on the research method chosen. In survey research, a lone researcher would simply not have the time to carry out large numbers of face-to-face interviews and process the resulting data. In ethnography, a lone researcher can only become involved with a relatively small group of people, or a clearly delimited social context such as a classroom. If labour power is in short supply the research is likely to take the form of a small survey, or a case-study, or perhaps be based on secondary data.

Time and labour power usually boil down to a matter of money. If there is enough money to pay salaries, either more time can be taken or a larger research team created, which can do the same amount of work more quickly. Clearly, the larger the team that can be trained to administer an interview schedule, the larger the sample that can be questioned. In the case of ethnography, the financial question is largely a matter of how long the researcher's salary and living expenses can be met. If there is plenty of money, then a team of ethnographers can work together, as in Becker's studies (Becker *et al.* 1961, 1968), or in the Banbury restudy (Stacey 1975). The question of the funding of research was discussed on p. 11.

Gaining access to a group of respondents whom you wish to interview or administer questionnaires to, or getting into a group you wish to observe can also be a serious practical problem. Sociologists need to ask themselves whether the research population is accessible, whether it is deviant and therefore suspicious of the motives of researchers, whether it is literate or illiterate, and whether it is concentrated in one place or geographically dispersed. Difficulty of access to a sample might mean that a preferred method (in-depth interviewing, for example) would have to be changed (perhaps to questionnaires). This is not uncommon when the issue is a sensitive one, such as deviant sexual behaviour, or mental illness.

Joining exclusive or deviant groups which tend to shut out 'outsiders' or gaining access to them to conduct questionnaires and interviews is not impossible but needs to be sensitively thought through in terms of both ethics and personal safety. Very often, the sociologist will need to use an intermediary, or 'gate-keeper' – a person who does have contact with a relevant or appropriate set of individuals. For example, access to victims of domestic violence is not easy. An intermediary is crucially important for the sociologist, since s/he can perhaps vouch for the researcher and help establish a bond of trust between the sociologist and the group in question. Key professionals can sometimes fill this role, e.g. social workers can often introduce a researcher to women who have been abused.

Finally, the nature of the subject matter can affect the choice of method. Some subjects are very sensitive, e.g. people may not admit willingly to behaviour such as domestic violence, racism or certain types of sexual behaviour. Consequently, researchers need to think carefully about what research methods are going to produce the most valid data.

There is a four-cornered relationship between theoretical preferences, choice of topic (discussed on pp. 10–11), practical considerations, and choice of research method, as shown in Figure 1.2.

Figure 1.2 Choice of research topic

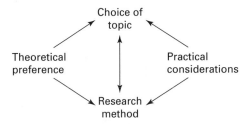

A sociologist's theoretical perspective will guide the choice of topic and research method adopted. Choice of topic influences research method and vice versa. Time, money and labour power will in turn determine what is realistically possible.

2

Social surveys

A social survey is a method of obtaining large amounts of data, usually in a statistical form, from a large number of people in a relatively short time. It usually takes the form of a self-completion questionnaire (this may be handed to the respondent or sent through the post) or an interviewer may read the questions to the respondent and fill in the questionnaire (otherwise known as an 'interview schedule') on behalf of the respondent. If the latter course is taken, the survey method is termed a 'structured interview'. Whichever survey method is used, the social survey has for many years been the most widely used method of social research. Such surveys aim to be explanatory or descriptive and, sometimes, a combination of these.

The investigations into poverty carried out by Peter Townsend (1957, 1979) were both descriptive and explanatory, and were intended to prompt governments into modifying their policies in relation to the poor. The series of British Crime Surveys

(Mayhew and Mirlees-Black 1993; Mirlees-Black *et al.* 1996, 1998) set out to describe the extent of crime in Britain. The crime surveys carried out in Merseyside and Islington, by contrast, are designed to be explanatory and to predict who is most at risk (Kinsey *et al.* 1985; Jones *et al.* 1986; Pearce 1990).

Sociologists working within the positivist scientific tradition particularly advocate the use of the social survey. The survey method is regarded as scientific because surveys are normally carried out under controlled conditions. They are organized in a logical and systematic fashion via questionnaire design. If the research is properly carried out, the personal influence of the researcher on the results is slight. In other words, they are seen to be objective and value-free. Very importantly, they are regarded as highly reliable because they are easily replicated and the quantifiable data can be verified by others. Moreover, the survey produces large amounts of statistical information, relatively quickly and cheaply, which enables comparisons to be made between different groups and populations. Surveys are also appealing because they can be aimed at large groups of people thus making them more representative of wider society.

On the other hand, qualitative researchers argue that social surveys with their emphasis on scientific logic and statistical data give us little insight into how people see and understand their lives. Surveys are seen as artificial devices that produce artificial responses in that 'approaching respondents like this creates a thoroughly unnatural situation, so whatever the results, they won't have much bearing on what respondents usually think, generally feel, normally experience, or really believe' (Gomm 2004: 156).

Stages in a survey

The stages in a survey are:

1 choosing the topic to be studied
2 reviewing the literature

3 forming of hunches and hypotheses
4 identifying the population to be surveyed
5 carrying out preparatory investigations and interviews
6 drafting the questionnaire or interview schedule
7 conducting a pilot survey
8 finalizing the questionnaire
9 selecting a sample of the population
10 selecting and training interviewers (if necessary)
11 collecting the data
12 processing the data and analysing the results
13 writing the research report, perhaps in the form of a book
14 publication of the report.

At this point, however, it must be stressed that there is always a difference between what textbooks say and what real research is actually like. The stages are listed here not because this is exactly what every survey is like, or should be like, but because survey researchers have to consider all these points at some stage, and usually in roughly this order. To develop an understanding of what survey research is actually like, you should read studies in the original.

We will now consider each stage in turn.

Choice of topic to be studied   Some of the reasons why researchers choose their topics have been discussed in Chapter 1. Normally, of course, the choice of topic comes before the research design and therefore also precedes the decision about whether or not to include a survey. As already mentioned, a survey is done where the researcher wishes to gather large amounts of data from a relatively large number of people. But there are certain topics which simply cannot be studied by this method. Many historical themes are an example, since no respondents (people who answer the questions) are available. Illiterate people cannot be given a questionnaire, though they may, of course, be interviewed. A study of the distribution of power in society as a whole could hardly use the survey method, for who would be questioned and what questions could be asked? People who have something to hide, such as criminals or deviants, or even ordinary school pupils, may deliberately give untrue answers in order to protect themselves.

Reviewing the literature Every researcher, of whatever status, should spend time reading what other people have written about the area in which they are interested. This will involve a systematic search through library catalogues and perhaps online journals, and has several purposes. First, it can give ideas about research design, key issues and methods of data collection. Second, it may identify problems in the research proposal and save the researcher repeating another's mistakes. Third, it is part of the process of increasing human knowledge that every contribution builds on, or at least relates to, previous work. (See Bell (2000) for some helpful suggestions.)

Forming of hypotheses Most survey researchers will present an explicit hypothesis and set out to test it. An hypothesis is an informed guess about what the researcher thinks may be happening, based on previous reading, research and observation. This hypothesis will be broken down into a number of indicators which can be operationalized, i.e. turned into questions which collect evidence that may support or challenge the hypothesis.

Identification of the population to be surveyed In some cases, this will be easy. If we are interested in the political opinions of young people, then all we have to do is to decide what age group we are interested in, and our population consists of all those people. If we wish to investigate the political opinions of students in higher education, then that is our research population.

What if, however, we want to investigate the impact that a new motorway has had on the surrounding area? Whom do we ask? Everybody who lives in the area? Including the children aged four or five? Should we include people who have moved away because of the motorway? If so, how can we identify and trace them? Perhaps we should include people who work in the area but do not live there? Should we not include people who regularly travel through the area by car, who must have an opinion about the difference it has made to their journey? And what about the local shopkeepers, or owners of cafés and petrol stations? Should they not be investigated as a special category of people affected? How big an area are we going to investigate? Will we not have to make a decision in advance of what the extent of the motorway's influence has been?

You may think that you have answers to all these questions, and no doubt you have. What you must recognize is that the answers given to the questions will affect the outcome of the research. It follows that, when reading the reports of studies such as this, it is essential to be clear about the choices that the researcher made when deciding on the population to be surveyed.

Carrying out preparatory investigations and interviews This is not always done, but some researchers who may not have formed clear and focused hypotheses spend time at this early stage in conducting informal or discovery interviews with people in order to find out from them what the key issues are. (See, for example, Mirlees-Black *et al.* 1996 ; Jowell *et al.* 1999; Marshall *et al.* 1988.) For example, if a researcher wants to investigate the factors that influence pupils when they are choosing the subjects they wish to study at higher levels of education, then group discussions with, for example, fourteen-year-old pupils in almost any secondary school would give some ideas about what questions to include in a questionnaire. The researcher could not draw any generally valid or reliable conclusions from such discussions, but they should provide useful guidelines as to what areas should be followed up in the main enquiry.

Drafting the questionnaire or interview schedule A questionnaire is a list of questions to be asked by the researcher. It is prepared in such a manner that the questions are asked in exactly the same way of every respondent. It may be administered in a number of ways. It may be completed by the respondent whilst the researcher waits or it may be sent through the post, or included in, for example, a newspaper or magazine, when it will be completed by the respondent without any supervision or guidance. It may be sent online via e-mail (see p. 66).

A questionnaire that is administered face-to-face by a researcher is known as an 'interview schedule' and is part of a 'structured interview'. Often, the interviewer is able to exercise little or no discretion as to how to ask the questions or in what order. However, some surveys use semi-structured interviews which do allow some flexibility and discretion, within a framework that is similar on every occasion. Where the form and order of an interview is left very much to the interviewer, we are dealing with an 'unstructured interview'. Interview schedules, then, can fall anywhere on a scale from the completely structured to the completely unstructured, and many include questions of several types within the same schedule. The structured interview is favoured by researchers who attach great importance to the objective scientific status of the research method and process, whilst the unstructured interview is preferred by those sociologists interested in uncovering the social meanings that lie behind social action.

When deciding what questions to ask, the researcher's first problem is usually to 'operationalize' the concepts to be used. This essentially means converting the hypothesis and related concepts into question form. As so often in sociology, this rather alarming-sounding process is really very simple, though difficult to do well.

The problem is that most of the things that sociologists are interested in are abstract. They are concepts rather than actual objects. If I want to count how many chairs there are in my college, I have little problem about deciding which of the many objects in college I am going to include in my count. If, on the other hand, I want to count how many working-class students there are in the college, I cannot just go ahead and do it. I have to decide what I mean by 'working-class', and then I have to choose an 'indicator' of this concept. This indicator must be a characteristic that is easily identifiable, and which clearly distinguishes working-class students from others. Most sociologists faced with this particular problem have used occupation or level of educational achievement as the indicator. They do not claim that occupation or education is the same thing as social class, but rather that it is the best single indicator of all those aspects of a person that make up their social class position. Consequently, sociologists and also civil servants have produced social class scales which put professional people at the top, then other non-manual workers, then various grades of manual worker. The best example of this in recent years was the classification of occupations used by the government, i.e. the Registrar-General's scale which is a hierarchy of occupations loosely based on education, income and status.

Not everybody agreed with this method of operationalizing 'social class'. For example, critics of the Registrar-General's classification were unhappy that it was based solely on male occupations and that females were categorized according to the job of their husband, or if unmarried, their father. People without jobs, e.g. those who live off wealth, or the never-employed unemployed were excluded from the classification. There were also very large variations in income within particular social class categories. Moreover, a good dual income might mean that a couple classified as Social Class III Non Manual might have a better income and lifestyle than a couple classed as Social Class I.

In general, then, it was agreed that the Registrar-General's classification was unsatisfactory. In 2001, it was replaced by the National Statistics Socio-Economic Classification which is also based on employment but is no longer focused exclusively on skill levels. Rather it is based on (a) employment relations, i.e. whether people are employers, self-employed or

Figure 2.1 The Registrar-General's social class scheme

Class 1: Professional
Accountant, architect, barrister, chemist, company director, company secretary, doctor, engineer, judge, solicitor, university lecturer

Class 2: Intermediate
Chiropodist, farmer, laboratory technician, librarian, manager, Member of Parliament, nurse, police officer, social worker, publican, teacher

Class 3NM: Skilled non-manual
Cashier, clerical worker, draughtsman, estate agent, secretary, shop assistant, travelling salesman, typist, waiter

Class 3M: Skilled manual
Baker, bus driver, butcher, bricklayer, carpenter, electrician, miner, plumber, policeman, train driver

Class 4: Semi-skilled
Agricultural labourer, barman, factory machinist, postman, telephone operator

Class 5: Unskilled
Car park attendant, cleaner, docker, labourer, refuse collector, road sweeper

Source: adapted from Reid 1989: 56.

employed, and if the latter, whether they exercise authority at work, and (b) employment market conditions, i.e. salary, promotion prospects, whether they receive benefits such as sick pay, and how much control they exercise over their job in terms of hours worked or how the work is done. Critics have pointed out that this has now resulted in a complex classification made up of eight social classes which is difficult to apply in practice under research conditions. Some researchers, consequently, have made the decision to stick with the familiar Registrar-General's scale (e.g. Power *et al.* 2003) or to construct variations on that theme. Jesson *et al.* (1992) used father's current or last occupation but mother's occupation in the absence of a father. They also operationalized 'poverty'

Figure 2.2 The National Statistics Socio-Economic Classifications (NS–SEC)

---

1 Higher managerial and professional occupations

   1.1 **Employers and managers in larger organizations**
company directors, senior company managers, senior civil servants, senior officers in police and armed services

   1.2 **Higher professionals**
doctors, lawyers, clergy, librarians, teachers and social workers

2 Lower managerial and professional occupations
nurses and midwives, journalists, actors, musicians, prison officers, lower ranks of police and armed forces

3 Intermediate occupations
clerks, secretaries, driving instructors, telephone fitters

4 Small employers and own account workers
publicans, farmers, taxi drivers, window cleaners, painters and decorators

5 Lower supervisory, craft and related occupations
printers, plumbers, television engineers, train drivers, butchers

6 Semi-routine occupations
shop assistants, hairdressers, postal workers, bus drivers, cooks

7 The never-employed and long-term unemployed

Source: adapted from Langley 1999: 35.

in schools by examining the percentage of pupils receiving free school meals.

Once the hypothesis and its related concepts have been broken down into indicators, it is possible to begin drafting questions. The skills involved are so varied and complex that whole books have been written about it, and there is no chance of going into the topic in great depth here. There are, however, some points to be made.

Questionnaires or interview schedules may be made up of 'closed' or 'open' questions. With the use of closed questions, the researcher has in some way limited the possible responses.

For example, there may be a simple yes/no/don't know set of alternatives to choose from. Or there may be a list of possible answers, of which at least one must be ticked. The advantage of this method is that results can be presented in the form of statistics and tables. This requires that answers be pre-coded so that the responses can be fed straight into a computer which has been programmed to receive them. The problem is that the researcher has imposed a limit on the possible answers that the respondent may give, and this may cast doubt on the validity of the data collected.

Sometimes questionnaires which are composed of closed questions will use scaling devices such as the Likert scale to produce a comparative set of data based on strength of feeling or belief. In other words, respondents will be asked to tick one from a range of boxes indicating 'very strongly agree', 'agree', 'have no opinion', 'disagree' and 'strongly disagree'. Similar questions may focus on asking people levels of satisfaction on, say, a scale of one to five.

With open questions the researcher leaves it to the respondents as to how they word their answers. Questions can therefore be more wide-ranging and open-ended. Such questions are more often asked in the interview situation than in a postal questionnaire. The interviewer may ask a question and follow it up with 'prompts' or 'probes' to encourage the respondents to go into more depth with their answers. There are, however, dangers in 'over-probing', which may put answers into respondents' heads.

Open questions make it possible for respondents to say what they really feel, but it is difficult for the researcher to organize the answers into categories in order to count them. With closed questions it is easier to count the replies and perform statistical operations on them, but it is difficult to get at what the respondent really thinks about something. Many interviews are semi-structured in that they have a mix of the two types of questions. They may start with closed questions about, for example, age or marital status, and move on to more open-ended questions as the interview progresses.

The wording of questions, especially closed questions and those asked in a postal questionnaire, must be clear, precise and unambiguous. The language used should be as simple as possible. Questions must not presume that respondents have more knowledge than in fact they have, and must not lead respondents towards a particular answer. Questions must not be loaded with emotion so that the respondent is forced down a particular path in order to avoid what they see as a negative judgement of their behaviour. Jargon and vague words like 'few', 'several' and 'generally' should be avoided because people may not share the same interpretation of their meaning. Question design, therefore, requires a great deal of skill and practice.

As an example of the pitfalls involved in drafting questions, we can consider the fuss that there was in 1983 when Hill announced that he had found that as many as 40 per cent of six-year-old children had seen 'video-nasties' (i.e. video films of horror, violence and sadistic sex). In his questionnaire, he named some of the more famous of such videos, and asked the children to say whether they had seen them. His findings produced a lively press response, and questions in the House of Commons, and certainly contributed to the passage of a bill through Parliament to limit the availability of such films. Cumberbatch and Bates repeated the research, asking another sample of children, eleven-year-olds this time, whether they had seen certain such videos. They achieved a figure of 68 per cent of the children claiming to have seen these films. The point was, however, that Cumberbatch and Bates had named a number of video-nasties that did not in fact exist, and yet the children claimed that they had seen them. What Hill had found was that children claimed to have seen video-nasties, rather than had actually seen them. This is a very good example of the validity problem referred to on pp. 9–10.

Figure 2.3 Questions in social surveys

Secondary schooling

I want to ask you about your schooling *after* the age of eleven.
What schools did you go to then? (Any others?)

circle all
which apply

Stayed at exact same school 01
Elementary school 02
Central/Intermediate/Higher elementary/Senior school 03
All-age school/Advanced division 04
Secondary modern/Junior secondary school/
    Vocational school (Republic of Ireland-South) 05
Comprehensive (including multilateral and bilateral
    schools) 06
Technical school 07
   ⌜ Grammar school . . . . 08 ⎦ give
      Direct grant/Grant aided 09   name(s)
      Independent (fee-paying) school 10   and
   ⌞ Scotland only: senior secondary school . . . 11 ⎦ location(s)
      Scotland only: higher grade 12
      Republic of Ireland only:
        'secondary' school 13

(*Source*: Halsey, Heath and Ridge 1980)

Your marriage

(a) How did you meet your husband? . . . .
(b) What was the date of your marriage? . . . .
    How old were you then? . . . .
(c) How many children have you? . . . .
(d) What are their ages? . . . .
(e) How many more children do you *expect* to have? . . . .
(f) Ideally, how many children would you *like* to have? . . . .

continued

Comment

(g) How do you see yourself now? Please tick one place on the following scale opposite each statement.

     1 = Essentially so
     2 = Very much so
     3 = To a large extent
     4 = To a certain extent
     5 = Not really

Someone who is:

		1	2	3	4	5	
1	providing an interesting activity for your children						1
2	creating a comfortable and well-run home						2
3	a companion to your husband						3
4	concerned with interests of your own, e.g. pottery						4
5	keen to do a paid job now and again						5
6	keen to follow a career of your own						6
7	active in local clubs, church, or other organizations						7
8	a friendly person in your neighbourhood						8

(*Source*: Pahl and Pahl 1971)

Couples

1   In our society some people claim that equality between the sexes has been achieved. Do you agree?.................

2   Would your briefly explain why you agree or disagree in Question 1 above.....................................

3 Do you think that equality between the sexes in all walks of life is a good thing or a bad thing? . . . .

4 Would you briefly explain why you think that equality between the sexes is a good or bad thing? . . . .

5 How do you regard domesticity? Please delete any inappropriate words.

   Easy/difficult/boring/interesting/worthwhile/waste of time/enjoyable/unenjoyable/satisfying/unsatisfying

6 Whose company do you prefer most? Please delete any inappropriate words.

   Relatives/friends/professional colleagues/males/females

7 If you were granted three wishes, what would you wish for? Please be as specific as possible and put them in order of importance.

   (a) . . . .

   (b) . . . .

   (c) . . . .

Please try and answer all the following questions as frankly as possible. This is of the highest importance if the survey findings are to be valid. There are no 'right' or 'wrong' answers. Please indicate your answers by marking the response which most accurately fits your own experience.

1 Do you and your mate agree on how your children should be brought up?

   Always agree/almost always agree/occasionally agree/ occasionally disagree/almost always disagree/always disagree

2 Do you and your mate agree on the type of education your children should receive?

   Always agree/almost always agree/occasionally agree/ occasionally disagree/almost always disagree/always disagree

continued

3 Do you and your mate agree on the subject of contraception?

Always agree/almost always agree/occasionally agree/occasionally disagree/almost always disagree/always disagree

(*Source*: Edgell 1980)

Church attendance

12 Please estimate the average number on a typical Saturday/Sunday in September 1998 at this church. (Please count any adults or children who attend more than one Saturday/Sunday service once only.)

Total number of adults (aged 15 or above) . . . .

Total number of children (aged 14 or under). . . . .

13 We appreciate that it is difficult but it would be a great help if you could estimate the approximate numbers of your total adult congregation who attend Saturday/Sunday services on a weekly, fortnightly, monthly and less frequent basis.

Twice weekly . . . . . Weekly . . . . . Fortnightly . . . . .

Monthly . . . . . Quarterly . . . . . . Twice a year . . . . .

14 Please could you estimate the approximate numbers of your congregation who attend Saturday/Sunday services who fall into the following age-groups:

Under 15 . . . . . . 15–19 . . . . . 20–9 . . . . . . 30–44 . . . . .

45–64 . . . . . 65 and over . . . . .

15 Please could you estimate the approximate numbers in your congregation who fall into the following ethnic groups:

Black Caribbean/African/Black Other . . . . . .

Chinese/Korean/Japanese . . . . . Indian/Pakistani/

Bangladeshi . . . . . Other Asian . . . . . Other non-white . . . . . .

(*Source*: English Church Attendance Survey 1998, cited in Brierley 2003)

Asian adolescents

Please answer these questions by putting an 'X' next to the statement that applies to you, or filling in the blank.

5   At home we speak only English

   At home we speak only our Asian language

   At home we speak both English and our Asian language

6   What is your father's job? . . . .

7   What is your mother's job, if she has one outside
   the home? . . . .

8   Please state the religion of your family. . . . .

Below you will find a number of statements about Asians living in Britain. I would like to know YOUR OWN VIEWS on these topics. Please answer by circling ONE response for each question. SA means STRONGLY AGREE, A means AGREE, U means UNSURE/DON'T KNOW, D means DISAGREE, and SD means STRONGLY DISAGREE.

1   Girls and boys should be treated the same

   SA A U D SD

2   Schools should accept our traditional clothes

   SA A U D SD

4   I have no wish to go back to live in the country
   my parents come from

   SA A U D SD

5   I would like to see boys and girls from our community
   going out with English boys and girls

   SA A U D SD

(*Source*: Ghuman 1999)

Despite these potential problems, the questionnaire is highly valued by researchers particularly those who believe in scientific method because they are standardized and so everybody who fills one in is subjected to the same stimulus. Moreover positivists also see questionnaires which use closed questions as more reliable than most other research methods because the sociologist should be able to repeat the questionnaire elsewhere on similar samples of people and get much the same sorts of results. The questionnaire also allows the researcher the possibility of using larger numbers of respondents than any other method available, therefore increasing the representativeness of the sample and the ability to generalize from the results.

Distributing questionnaires is a reasonably quick way of conducting research especially if questions are mainly of the closed variety. Such questions are customer-friendly because they take less time and effort to complete and consequently they are less likely to result in refusal and non-response. Some sociologists argue that personal and embarrassing questions which may be negatively influenced by the fact of being face-to-face with someone in an interview may be more likely to be answered as part of a questionnaire. Questionnaires also involve minimal interaction with the researcher and therefore there is seen to be less opportunity for subjective bias caused by factors such as power relations and status differences to undermine the validity of the data collected. Finally, the quantifiable nature of the questionnaire is seen as attractive because statistical data can be comparatively analysed and correlated.

However, some sociologists, especially those working within the ethnographic tradition are sceptical about the uses of the questionnaire. Interpretivist sociologists argue that since the questions are pre-coded this reduces the chances of uncovering the real meanings behind the actions or behaviour of social actors. For example, the opinions, attitudes and experiences of people in everyday social life may be too complex to fit within a narrow 'box' or set of categories, and therefore the answers the respondent may want to give may not appear as an option on the survey. This may create frustration and therefore non-response or result in false or distorted, i.e. invalid, data being collected. Even if the answer a respondent wanted to give was present on the list of options, it is argued that true meanings may still not be uncovered because when different people tick the same box, they may not share the meaning of that option. Take the question, 'do you think the prime minister has too much power?' – the word 'power' mean different things in the context of that question to different people, power over the country, power over the Labour Party, power over foreign policy and so on. Unless the researcher has made a concerted effort to make sure all respondents share absolutely his or her meaning, questionnaire data will always suffer from this 'problem of meaning'.

Interpretivists are also sceptical about the positivist claim that questionnaires are an objective method. They point out that questionnaires with closed questions reflect and impose the researcher's own values and priorities on to respondents. The researcher has decided not only what questions are relevant and important to ask, but also the range of responses that can come out of the data. Closed questions assume that the sociologist knows all the possible answers and that any alternatives which the respondent experiences are unimportant. Respondents may therefore feel forced into making responses with which they don't really agree. Alternatively, they may feel frustrated with, even alienated from, the research and withdraw their cooperation.

Conducting a pilot survey This stage of questionnaire-based research should never be omitted. In it, the researcher tries out the questionnaire on a number of people who are similar to those who will be investigated in the actual research. Any problems with the wording of the draft questionnaire should show up at this stage and can be corrected before the real investigation starts. With a postal questionnaire, it is important to check that the layout is not confusing or encouraging a particular response.

Finalizing the questionnaire   At this point the researcher will produce a final version of the questionnaire, ready for use in the real investigation.

Further reading

The following books include copies of the full questionnaires that were used:

Pahl and Pahl (1971); Edgell (1980); Heath et al. *(1985); Mack and Lansley (1985); Marshall* et al. *(1988); Saunders (1990); Finch and Mason (1993); Gregson and Lowe (1994); Wellings* et al. *(1994), Ghuman (1999). The Centre for Applied Social Surveys (CASS) has a question bank containing dozens of survey questionnaires which students and teachers can access by going to www.natcen.ac.uk/cass or www.qb.soc.surrey. ac.uk*

Selecting a sample of the population   In this context, the term 'population' refers to all those people who could be included in the survey. As we have already seen (pp. 31–2), this may be quite clear, or it may require decisions to be made about who will be included and who will be omitted. Either way, the chances are that there will be a very large number of people, possibly several million, depending on the subject of the research, and there is no way that the researcher is going to be able to deliver a questionnaire to them all, still less interview them face to face. Accordingly, a sample has to be chosen.

We are all familiar with the idea of sampling. For example, when I go to the market to buy fruit, I will usually, despite what the stall-holder says, try to handle an apple or two from the display to see what they are like. If I am happy with their quality, I will ask for the quantity that I want. I assume that the quality of the ones I have handled is typical or representative of the quality of the others. When I dip my toe in the swimming pool before going in, I assume that the temperature of that part of the water is representative of the temperature of the whole pool.

Exactly the same principle applies when sampling for social research. The researcher aims to investigate a sample of the population, because this is cheaper and quicker, but the sample must be representative of the population as a whole. That is to say, what is true of the sample should be true of the population, or at least it should be possible to calculate the likelihood of its being true. There are various ways of selecting such a sample.

'Random' or 'probability' sampling is the one with which most people are familiar. The researcher first has to produce a 'sampling frame'. This is a list of the population concerned, organized into 'sampling units'. Choosing a sampling unit may itself be a problem. If we are interested only in individuals, it is a straightforward matter. But what if we want to investigate families? Or households? These will need to be defined, and then some means of assembling a list of them will have to be found.

However, let us assume that we are interested in individuals. There are various lists available for this purpose. If we are investigating adults, then a common sampling frame used by sociologists is the electoral register (Marshall *et al.* 1988). This is the list of all those in an area who are eligible to vote at elections. It is brought up to date each year, and includes virtually everybody over eighteen who is resident in a constituency. General practitioner's lists of patients may be another possible sampling frame. In recent years, the Post-code Address File (PAF) has become available to researchers. If we are studying school-pupils in a certain area, then we might try to get hold of a list of all secondary school attendees from the local education office or schools in that area. If we are interested in young mothers, then we might try the Register of Births, and ask for a list of all recent births that have been registered.

Such lists are not always easy to find, as is described by Newby (1977) when he tried to devise a sampling frame of farms in a certain area. They may not exist or access to them may be refused. Pearson (1981) found that:

> In common with previous studies of ethnic minorities in Britain, it proved difficult to find a suitable sampling frame . . . Electoral registers, street directories, etc., were either inappropriate (these lists do not indicate birth-place or nationality) or unavailable (for example, Council housing or rating lists). A sample was finally constructed by using the files of a local vicar and a list of West Indian parents which was obtained from a local junior school.

Telephone directories have been used by some studies but these exclude people who are ex-directory or people who don't have phones and those who only have mobile phones. Some sociologists have reverted to using maps when no list has proved suitable. A couple of areas on a map might be randomly selected, then streets randomly selected within those areas and households randomly selected on those streets.

Once we have a sampling frame, we can select a certain number of names from it. If we choose names out of a hat, or by using random numbers, then we are doing truly random sampling. If we choose every tenth or every twentieth name, then this is called quasi-random sampling, since not every name on the list has an equal chance of being chosen.

Stratified sampling works slightly differently. It is always possible, though unlikely, that a random sample will, by chance, include a higher proportion of one group of people than there should be for it to be truly representative. If a town has 10,000 residents over the age of twenty-one, of whom exactly half are male and half female, a random sample of one tenth of them is unlikely to produce exactly half men and half women, and it might produce a very biased sample of, say, 650 women and 350 men. To avoid this possibility, we can opt for a stratified sample. In this case, we would divide our population into men and women, and then take a 10 per cent sample of each of these groups. In this way, we would be guaranteed to produce 500 men and 500 women. If we wanted further to stratify the sample to allow for age distribution, we could do this too, by dividing the men and the women into age groups, and taking one tenth of each of the resulting groups. In the early British Crime Surveys (Hough and Mayhew 1983, 1985) and the Islington Crime Survey (Jones *et al.* 1986) an 'ethnic minority booster sample' was included, to ensure that this significant group was properly represented.

Quota sampling is like stratified sampling, but with an important variation. In this case, the researcher decides how many of each category of person should be included in the sample, but then, instead of selecting them at random from a sampling frame, the researcher goes out looking for the right number of people in each category until the quota is filled. Thus if, in a sample of 500 people, the quota of women aged between thirty and forty is twenty-two, the researcher will look out for twenty-two such women and, when they have been found and interviewed, that is the quota filled. This method is most often used by market researchers, but is not unknown among sociologists. However, because it lacks randomness, there is a danger that bias might creep into the selection of the sample, i.e. researchers may only stop and question people who look 'suitable' or 'co-operative' and consequently the sample may not be representative of the research population. As Robson (2002) notes

if, for example, home visits are involved, avoiding houses where there is a Rottweiler or other large dog, or there are no curtains, or apartments where the lift is out of order, etc. may be understandable behaviour on the part of the sensitive interviewer, but militates against representativeness in householders in the sense of all householders having an equal chance of appearing in the sample.

(p. 264)

Multi-stage sampling just means drawing one sample from another. If we wanted a national sample of school-children, we could draw a sample of education authorities, then draw a sample of schools from each of those, then a sample of children from each school. Many of the studies conducted by Social and Community Planning Research use a multi-stage sample of parliamentary constituencies, polling districts, addresses, and individuals (e.g. Jowell *et al.* 1985, 1986, 1987, 1988).

'Purposive sampling' occurs when a researcher chooses a particular group or place to study because it is known to be of the type that is wanted. Goldthorpe and his team (1969) wanted to study manual workers with high incomes to see whether they had developed a middle-class way of life. They decided to study a group of workers in Luton because they were known to have high incomes. Goldthorpe thought that, if they had not adopted a middle-class way of life, then it was unlikely that any other working-class people had done so.

There are various other kinds of sampling procedure, and any statistics textbook will explain them. Another one you may come across is known as 'snowball' sampling. This is much less systematic than the others described above, and has little claim to be representative at all. It is used in ethnographic research more than in surveys. It involves identifying certain key individuals in a population, interviewing them, and then asking them to suggest others who might also be interviewed. In this way, the original small nucleus of people grows by adding people to it in stages, much as a snowball can be built up by rolling it along the snow on the ground. This type of sampling tends to be applied to deviant or criminal groups that are difficult to access for research purposes. Maguire and Bennett's (1982) study of burglars asked the Governor of the local prison to let it be known that they were studying house burglars. One or two prisoners volunteered and this led to the prison grapevine spreading the news that the sociologists were harmless. They were able to conduct forty interviews in all.

Selection and training of interviewers (if necessary)   If there are large numbers of people to be interviewed, it will be necessary to select and train a team of people to act as assistant interviewers (e.g. Jowell *et al.*). The idea is that all the interviews should be conducted in as similar a way as possible, and that the dangers of 'interviewer effect' should be avoided by training. Interviewers have to strike a careful balance between establishing the kind of relationship with respondents that will encourage them to be frank and truthful, and avoiding becoming too friendly so that respondents try hard to please. 'Friendly but restrained' is a phrase often used to describe this attitude, and interviewers are usually encouraged to be as non-directive as possible. Becker, on the other hand, who tended to use a more open-ended style of interviewing, argued that the interviewer should sometimes 'play dumb' and pretend not to understand what is being said, in order to prompt the respondent into saying more. Some of these issues are explored in greater detail on pp. 59–64.

Collecting the data As we have seen, a questionnaire can be sent by post or administered face to face. Occasionally, a simple questionnaire may even be administered by telephone.

Money is usually important. Postal questionnaires are cheap to administer, and can cover very large numbers of people. Face-to-face interviews take time and cost much more in relation to the number of respondents interviewed.

There are several issues here. The first is the question of the 'response rate', which refers to the number of people who actually complete and return the questionnaire. This is the major drawback of the postal method, where response rates, usually around 30–40 per cent, are lower than in face-to-face research, which can hope to achieve a 70 or even 80 per cent response. Those to whom the questionnaire is sent have already been carefully selected as representative of the population to be studied. If some or even most of them do not respond, how can we know whether the answers that we have got are representative? Did people refuse to co-operate, or were they uncontactable, having moved or died? If some kind of bias has been introduced, how can we know what it is? Are people who volunteer to answer questionnaires in some way different from those who refuse? Are such differences important for this particular piece of research? All researchers have a system of calling back to respondents, and some will, in the end, use replacements, but this is another potential problem area.

In the end there is no answer to this problem, and it is very important, when evaluating published research, to take note of the response rate, and to consider whether it is adequate.

The second issue has two aspects: anonymity and confidentiality. With some research topics, such as asking people to say what criminal offences they have committed, the only chance of getting any truthful answers would be with a guarantee that the answers would be confidential (no one else would be told the answers given by a particular individual), and the best way of ensuring this is to allow respondents not to give their names (anonymity). This does not, of course, guarantee truthfulness, but it must improve the chance that the replies will be honest.

Processing the data and analysing the results Having collected all the completed questionnaires or interview schedules, it is time to process the data, putting answers into categories, adding up totals, and generally finding out the pattern of the responses and expressing them in statistical terms. Nowadays, computers can play a crucial role in this. In fact, they have made it possible to process far greater amounts of data than ever before.

Writing the research report, perhaps in the form of a book This can be a very lengthy process, depending on the amount of work that has to be done on the data collected. It is rare for any substantial report to be published within less than two years of the end of the data-collection phase, and it is very often a great deal longer than this. Even if the researcher completes the writing within, say, a year, publishers need up to a year to publish the book. It is not unusual for a researcher to 'trail' the main publication by means of articles in the learned journals.

Publication of the report Publication day is when the work becomes available to other social scientists. They will make judgements as to the quality of the work, basing their opinion upon what is actually published, and the author's reputation may be made or broken by what the critics say. This is an important aspect of research. It may be done partly for the love of the work, but every author is also concerned to establish a reputation for good work among those whose opinion matters.

Longitudinal studies

One of the problems of sociological research, especially survey style research, is that it is a snapshot of the social context which it is studying. It is, therefore, difficult to provide a sense of history or of social change. The longitudinal study is an attempt to respond to this problem. One version of this is the 'panel study'.

The usual procedure is for a sample, which is then referred to as the 'panel', to be selected in the usual random way, as described on p. 46, and for data about this sample to be collected at regular intervals over a period of years. The best way to show what this involves is by examples.

A good example of a longitudinal study is the National Child Development Study which has been following the development of all the children born in Britain in the week 3–9 March, 1958. Their first major report was *11,000 Seven Year Olds* published in 1966. Davie *et al.* published *From Birth to Seven* in 1972; it is a study of the health, education, and home environment of the children, and attracted a good deal of attention. Fogelman commented on the same group of children in regards to their adolescence in 1983.

Another more recent example of this approach is the work of the Child Health and Education Survey. This is a study of children born in the second week of April, 1970. Over 16,500 were born, and 13,135 were traced and studied in 1975. The most striking finding is the enormous range of social and economic circumstances in which children are brought up (Osborn *et al.* 1984; Osborn and Milbank 1987).

The British Household Panel Survey started in 1991 and is a multi-purpose study that follows the same representative sample of individuals – the panel – over a period of years. Its website at http://iserwww.essex.ac.uk/ulsc/bhps/ contains full details.

The Office of Population Censuses and Surveys (now the Office for National Statistics) started a longitudinal study in 1971 by selecting a 1 per cent sample from the Census returns. This sample is being traced through such sources as the Registrar of Births and Deaths, and was identified again in 1981, and has been identified in each Census since. Fox and Goldblatt, for example, have used the data to trace the relationship between illness and death rates and social class (Whitehead 1988). The UK data archive at www.data-archive. ac.uk contains information about and data from these and a number of other longitudinal surveys.

The advantages of longitudinal studies are that they make it possible to study change over time, though as a series of snapshots rather than as a continuous process.

There are several difficulties with longitudinal studies, in addition to the usual problems of sample-based survey research. First, it may be difficult to recruit a sample of people who know that they are taking on a very long-term commitment. Generally, people are rather flattered at the thought of being so important, but this may in turn create the problem that they become untypical because they know that they are in the sample, and will be questioned regularly about their lives, activities and attitudes.

Then there is the problem of keeping in touch with the sample. Members will die, move away, emigrate and perhaps change their minds about continuing with the work. Small children may have no choice about being included, but could develop strong feelings about it as they grow up and drop out. These problems will raise questions about the continuing representativeness of the sample. Are those who drop out, for whatever reason, untypical of the whole group? It may be possible to recruit new members to the panel, but this raises further questions.

The research team also needs to be held together. Work like this requires continuing enthusiasm of a kind that may not outlast the departure of the original members and their replacement with new people.

Lastly there is the question of cost, always important with social research, and particularly so here. Most funding agencies are, understandably, unwilling to take on a commitment to pay for research over a period of perhaps twenty years or more. Most of these studies have had a struggle to remain solvent, and have depended on the generosity of charitable foundations such as Nuffield and Ford, as well as finance from government agencies, often via the health services. In addition, they have made use of health visitors and others as free interviewers.

In addition to the panel version of longitudinal studies, surveys can be repeated at intervals though with different groups of respondents. This is the design of the annual series *British Social Attitudes* (e.g. Jowell *et al.* 1985–99) and of the *British Crime Survey* (e.g. Hough and Mayhew 1983, 1985; Mayhew *et al.* 1989; Mirlees-Black *et al.* 1998).

Before leaving the topic of longitudinal studies, it is worth pointing out that the Census can be seen as an example. Carried out every ten years since 1801, with the exception of 1941, it has most of the characteristics of the longitudinal survey except, of course, that it is a study of the whole population rather than a sample. Until recently, it has not been possible to use the Census to follow a particular group of people through their lives but it is perfectly feasible to study the changing population structure of, say, a particular district. It is invaluable to the sociologist who wishes to trace broad patterns of social change, and to make comparisons between the social conditions of one period and another (see also pp. 83–6).

Interviewing

It is useful at this stage to examine the interview method in a bit more depth because whilst it is an integral part of the social survey, it does have its own peculiar virtues and vices which are worth further investigation.

There are four broad types of interview used in social research. At one of the interviewing spectrum, we have the structured or formal interview which involves the researcher working through a series of standardized questions, i.e. an interview schedule or questionnaire. This type of interview is likely to be composed of closed questions and fixed choice responses. Structured interviews are mainly used to produce quantitative data. At the other end of the spectrum, we have the unstructured or informal interview which involves the researcher having a list of topic areas that need to be covered but there are no predetermined questions that have to be used. This interview is more like an informal conversation. Questions that are asked will tend to be open-ended and the emphasis will be on the respondent 'speaking for themselves'. In this sense, unstructured interviews mainly produce qualitative data. Semi-structured interviews tend to be made up of a combination of closed and open questions aimed at collecting both factual and attitudinal data.

Structured interviews are regarded highly by positivist researchers because, like questionnaires, they are standardized, respondents are exposed to the same questions or stimulus and data is usually quantifiable. Moreover, such interviews are capable of producing the same result when given to similar individuals. In other words, they are verifiable and therefore seen as a highly reliable methodological tool. Furthermore, they provide a large amount of straightforward factual and comparative information relatively cheaply.

However, interpretivist sociologists tend to be critical of structured interviews for the same reasons for which they are critical of questionnaires, i.e. they are critical of the use of closed questions in interview schedules. Interpretivists, as we saw earlier, argue that the use of closed questions and pre-coded answers devalues the experience of the respondent because it is effectively saying that unless the respondent has had an experience similar to the one mentioned in the interview schedule, the sociologist is not interested in them. In other words, the sociologist has already defined what experiences are important. In this sense, the sociologist is imposing their view of the world on the respondent rather than exploring the social reality of the interviewee. Interpretivists therefore argue that the content of a structured interview schedule may have little in common with the real world of the people it sets out to study. Dyer (1995) notes that highly structured interviews can feel, from the respondent's perspective, more like an interrogation, and consequently they are likely to elicit defensive rather than honest responses.

The unstructured interview

Interpretivists prefer the use of the unstructured interview in which the interviewer has some idea of the ground to be covered and the direction of the interview but has the liberty to change, and even abandon altogether, the question focus. Usually, the researcher is not confined by an interview schedule. Rather, he or she will have some idea of topics to be explored but will follow the interviewee if the researcher thinks it will generate interesting data. Questions are therefore not standardized. No two interviewees experience the same interview.

Unstructured interviews often use smaller samples than those found in large scale surveys. For example, Oakley's study of housework is based on intensive interviews with a sample of forty middle- and working-class women. Her interviews were completed in one session using a tape recorder and lasted between one and a quarter and three and a half hours. Often these types of interviews are used as part of an ethnographic approach as a means of supplementing data gathered by means of participant observation (see pp. 94–5) or to construct a life-history of an individual (see pp. 122–3).

Interpretivist sociologists argue that more in-depth information can be acquired using this type of interview. The use of smaller samples means that more time can be spent with respondents. This is useful because it allows time to develop a relationship of trust and rapport which may generate more qualitative information about people's beliefs, attitudes and interpretations of the world or on the respondent's past. For example, Willis in *Learning to Labour* (1977) includes many verbatim reports of his interviews with 'the lads' which give great insight into their interpretation of school, teachers, success and failure.

Rapport is assisted by the fact that unstructured interviews do not impose pre-set replies on respondents. In this sense, unstructured interviews provide an opportunity for respondents to say what they want rather than what the interviewer might expect. They can see that the sociologist values their input. The interviewer therefore avoids imposing his or her views on the interviewee. This may increase the validity of the research findings because the respondent may feel more comfortable with the interview situation and be more willing to open up. Thus this type of interviewing may be more likely to get at sensitive information difficult to reach using other methods. Unexpected, unanticipated and serendipitous responses may be forthcoming which reveal new lines of thinking in terms of relationships or hypotheses. Further probing by the interviewer is likely to uncover deeper meanings with regards to beliefs and attitudes which may be missed by more standardized methods. Darlington (1996) found in her study of women who had been sexually abused that by putting no constraints on the women in terms of the order in which topics were covered or how much they talked about it led to some of them volunteering that other forms of abuse such as verbal abuse and childhood putdowns had had more impact on their sense of self than sexual abuse.

On the other hand, those sociologists who argue for scientific principles to be the guiding force in sociological research claim that unstructured interviews have a number of important weaknesses. First, such interviews lack structure and standardization, and consequently the respondent may not focus enough on those aspects of the topic that interest the sociologist most. Second, it is claimed that it is an unreliable method because the data generated depends upon the unique relationship established between the interviewer and inter-viewee. Such data therefore is almost impossible to verify. In addition, such relationships may undermine objectivity. The possibility exists that somehow during the interview the interviewer influenced the respondent's perspective and responses in some way. Research using interviews also gen-erally involves small samples (because of the expense and the time-consuming nature of this method) so generalizations to wider populations may not be possible because of the unrepresentative nature of interview samples.

Interview effects

A number of problems have been identified with regard to the use of structured and unstructured interviews. The major problem with all types of interviews is interview effect (also known as interview bias). This problem stems from the fact that all interviews are interaction situations and this inevitably means that those who take part in them are attaching meanings or interpretations to what they see going on in them. We can illustrate this in a number of ways.

The status of the interviewer may be interpreted as threat-ening by the respondent. It is therefore important that status differences between the interviewer and interviewee be mini-mized as much as possible. Status refers to factors such as social class, ethnicity, gender, age or sexuality. For example, working-class respondents may interpret factors such as a suit and a BBC English accent as indicators of middle-class authority. They may feel patronized and consequently not be frank and honest with their interviewer. There is some evidence from Labov that working-class children may feel intimidated by middle-class teachers and consequently not communicate with them.

It may be inappropriate to have a male interviewer asking questions of a female respondent about sexual or domestic violence. A feminist critique of the British Crime Survey suggests that this survey fails to do justice to the real amount of sexual violence in society for this very reason. Hanmer and Saunders (1984), in their study of sexual violence in Leeds, made a point of only employing female interviewers who visited women on at least three occasions in order to gain their trust. The opposite problem can also occur. In a study of a social group characterized by masculine values it may be inappropriate to have female interviewers asking men about their lifestyles although some researchers do argue that a female may be seen as 'less threatening' than a male interviewer even in this situation.

Feminist researchers have tended to see unstructured interviewing as a uniquely female methodology. They reject the view that the researcher should be disengaged from the interviewee. They also argue that many interviews are hierarchical and exploitative. Unstructured interviews are seen as a means by which women can be given a voice in both sociology and society. Feminists therefore value engagement with their respondents and recommend that interviews be based on trust and emotional reciprocity Consequently feminists strongly argue that only women should interview other women. Scott (1990) and Finch (1984) give us some insight into the reasons why. Scott found that when she interviewed both male and female postgraduate students and university staff 'it sometimes felt that a different methodology was being used . . . when I interviewed women I struck up an immediate rapport . . . when it came to interviewing men . . . I found the same level of rapport impossible to achieve in most cases' (quoted in Hobson 1998). Finch, in her study of clergymen's wives suggests that women who spend most of their time in the home are more likely than men to welcome the opportunity to talk to a sympathetic listener. Moreover, women are more likely to cooperate than men with an unstructured interview because they are used to more intrusions in their lives through visits from doctors, health visitors and are less likely to interpret questions about their private lives as unusual. Finally, Fishman's (1990) study of interactions suggests men like to dominate conversation which may not be conducive to a successful interview.

There is some evidence that ethnic differences may create problems of validity. Ken Pryce in his study of West Indian and especially Rastafarian culture in *Endless Pressure* (1979) argues that being black himself increased the validity of his interview data especially with the Rasta group which sees white society as repressive. The research of Finkel *et al.* (1991) suggests that white respondents are less likely to express prejudice in the hearing of a black interviewer.

Bhatti (1999) notes that her status as an Asian woman researcher had a number of strengths and weaknesses in relation to her research into Asian children's experience of school. She notes that her sex and ethnicity as a Pakistani woman was a source of curiosity and suspicion for the white teachers she dealt with, especially when she talked to disruptive Asian children in Urdu and Punjabi. She notes when interviewing Asian parents that 'I sometimes took both my young children, neither of whom were school age, with me on home visits to the Asian parents. Most of the parents accepted my wife/mother persona as a homely non-threatening image' (p. 17). She found that Asian parents trusted her with confidential family matters once they realized she was bilingual.

Age may be another factor which affects the dynamics of an interview. Both Willis and Corrigan in their studies suggest that being in their early twenties when they conducted their interviews was advantageous in constructing trusting relationships with the adolescents whom they were studying. Labov argued that the interview may be interpreted as an 'asymmetrical power situation' by younger respondents and as such regarded as threatening.

Willmott (1966) chose to use young Australians and New Zealander interviewers in his research into the activities of adolescent boys, on the assumption that they would be seen by the boys as neutral as far as class and social background were concerned.

Where the interview is held may also affect the validity of the replies. In a survey of schoolchildren, we might expect that the answers they give in an interview held in the headmaster's study will be different from those they give at home, or out of doors. If the interview is at all long, the respondent must be comfortable and have time to answer the questions carefully.

Adams (2000) in her research on suspects' responses to rights when detained in police custody noted that dress can be an important factor in reducing barriers between interviewers and interviewees. Depending on whether she was interviewing suspects, solicitors or police officers, she 'dressed up' or 'dressed down' to manage the impression these three groups had of her.

> In interviews with suspects I wore blue jeans, pumps, and socks, a sweat shirt and no make-up. In interviews with police officers I wore a skirt, blouse, tights, shoes with a slight heel and a little make-up. In interviews with criminal defence solicitors I wore a two-piece Planet skirt suit, co-ordinated blouse, tights, shoes with a heel and make-up.
>
> (p. 391)

It is important that the interviewer's values, attitudes and opinions do not influence the respondent's answers. For example, interviewees may be able to tell the interviewer's opinion from the way the question is asked especially via the interviewer's facial expression or tone of voice. This may result in the interviewer 'leading' the respondent to a response that reflects the researcher's attitude and expectations.

Even those who do not feel threatened by the research will search for clues from the interviewer and the questions about how they ought to be behaving. These 'demand characteristics' can mean that respondents may be concerned about how the researcher sees them and consequently they may adjust their behaviour to what the respondent thinks the interviewer is after or demands. The 'social desirability' effect is one effect of demand characteristics. It involves the over-reporting of 'desirable' things such as giving to charity and the under-reporting of 'undesirable' things such as racist behaviour. Some respondents, therefore, may seek the approval of the interviewer by answering in ways which may be far from the truth. For example, research has shown that some ethnic groups are likely to mislead researchers regarding behaviour that their culture sees as deviant. Mental illness is a case in point. According to Dohrenwend and Dohrenwend (1969) Anglo-Saxons are less likely to admit to symptoms compared with Puerto Ricans. Dohrenwend concluded that this was because Puerto Rican society was more sympathetic to the problem whilst white Anglo-Saxon culture preferred to hide the problem away.

Another problem with interviews arises from human nature. Many people engage in yea-saying – they are so nice and so much want to cooperate with the interviewer that they prefer on balance to agree rather than disagree, to be satisfied rather than be dissatisfied etc.

The interview, therefore, can be interpreted as a very artificial situation. There is no guarantee that what people say in interviews is a true account of what they actually do, whether they are intentionally lying or whether they genuinely believe what they are saying. People are quite capable of saying one thing and doing another, and of being quite unaware of this. This can be illustrated by Aaron Cicourel's (1976) study of police behaviour. Cicourel interviewed police officers to see if they subscribed to stereotypical assumptions in their treatment of offenders from lower socio-economic groups. Police officers generally denied this and insisted that all juvenile offenders were treated in the same fashion. However, Cicourel's observation of officers on the beat discovered that social groups were treated differently. The officers, though, were genuinely unaware of the stereotypical nature of their actions. Interviews, therefore, do not allow the sociologists to directly observe people in their everyday environment. This may prevent the sociologist from discovering important aspects of people's behaviour.

The interviewer can be influenced by the interviewee (the respondent). The interviewer may form expectations about the interviewee on the basis of their age, social class, personality, demeanour, environment, etc. In other words, the interviewer may stereotype or label the interviewee as a certain 'type'. This becomes a problem if the researcher then makes sense of vague or ambiguous interview data in terms of their expectations about how these 'type' of people behave or think. The researcher may conclude that this 'type' of person was thinking along certain lines, whereas the interviewee might have meant something quite different.

All these problems of interview effect indicate that interview data depends upon how all the participants define the situation and their interpretations of each other. It is important that interviewers strike a careful balance between establishing trusting relationships which encourage respondents to be frank and truthful and avoiding introducing bias by becoming too friendly or subjective about the respondent.

Many of the above problems may be anticipated and resolved by carrying out pilot interviews to see how respondents respond to interviewing styles or by guaranteeing anonymity and confidentiality to respondents. Some studies have attempted to resolve some of these problems by using semi-structured interviews in order to obtain both quantitative and qualitative information. The latter type of data (i.e. verbatim quotations and descriptions) can be used to confirm the validity of the hard statistical data and the trends or correlations that come out of analysing these. Gregson and Lowe (1994) used semi-structured interviews with nannies and cleaners in their investigation of waged domestic labour in middle-class households.

Focus group interviews

Focus groups have been used for some years now in market research and have recently become more popular with sociologists, although Cohen and Taylor (1972) used group interviews in their study of long-term prisoners in the maximum security wing of a British prison, as did Taylor and Mullan (1986) when studying people's use of television.

These types of interview involve a group discussion led by a facilitator whose job is to manage the group dynamics by establishing trust and rapport in what people hopefully interpret as a secure, comfortable and confidential environment. The group is usually made up of 8–12 people. Focus group members are encouraged to talk to and respond to each other rather than to the facilitator, thus allowing people to explore their own attitudes and experiences in their own words. The group includes an 'observer' who notes the organization of the room and the dynamics of the interaction.

Focus groups not only measure the extent of an opinion; they can investigate the reasons why it was formed. They produce a good deal of qualitative data expressed in the words of the participants. For example, Loader *et al.* (1998) used focus groups with a range of citizens belonging to various age-groups to document levels of anxiety and fear about crime.

However, focus groups run into two main methodological problems. First, membership is not generally representative of particular social groups. As Gomm (2004) notes, people recruited into focus groups may be representative only of themselves. Focus groups may also not be representative of the general population because strong personalities may dominate discussion, influence less vocal members of the group and silence dissent. On the other hand, some researchers note that ethnic minority groups and children are more likely to feel supported and therefore will express themselves when they are surrounded by others like themselves. Gomm points out that focus groups can be useful for research which is focused on how people interact, behave and express themselves in group situations.

Telephone and online interviews

Two recent developments in interviewing have been telephone and on-line interviewing. Fielding and Thomas (2001) note that the telephone interview is increasingly used in social research. For example, Moran-Ellis and Fielding (1996) conducted such interviews with police-officers and social workers in their investigation of how official agencies dealt with child sex abuse. However, such interviews have weaknesses in that important visible clues such as body language and facial expression can no longer be observed. Also, there is such public hostility nowadays to telephone market research that a request for a telephone interview might not be positively received.

The most common type of on-line interviewing is administered through e-mail. Fielding and Thomas note that it lends itself well to cross-national research. Some researchers have accessed on-line 'chat rooms'. For example, Williams and Robson (2003) set up a virtual focus group in an on-line chat room in order to explore experiences of victimization. However, the major drawback of on-line interviewing is that you cannot verify the identity of the person who is responding. They may be 'playing a role' and consequently there are real doubts about the validity of the data being received.

Conclusions

We have seen that a good deal of the discussion above has been set in the context of quantitative and qualitative traditions. However, it is important that the distinction between these two models of social research is not over-stated. As Silverman (1997) notes, it aids our understanding of this topic to think in terms of a qualitative/quantitative divide, but the reality in terms of practical social research is the tendency to use a mixture of qualitative and quantitative techniques as part of a triangulation or methodological pluralism approach. For example, Ghazala Bhatti's (1999) study uses interviews with children, their parents and teachers, a closed questionnaire survey and participant observation inside and outside the classroom to construct an ethnographic account of Asian children at home and school. The use of such combinations of quantitative and qualitative methods has actually been the pragmatic norm for some time.

Further reading

The books listed on p. 46 all include a reasonably full description of how their survey was carried out, as do the following: Bott (1971); Jones et al. (1986); Jowell et al. (1985–99); Oakley (1979); Roberts et al. (1977); Schofield (1965); Willmott (1966); Young and Willmott (1957).

3

Experiments and the comparative method

When people think of natural scientists doing research, they tend to think of them in a laboratory, probably doing an experiment. The experiment is the classic research method of the natural scientist, and has produced many of its most valuable results, both in pure and in applied science. This is because the experiment is most suited to the assumptions that natural scientists have traditionally made about what they are studying. They assume that the natural world has an independent existence of its own, which is as it is regardless of those who are studying it, and which is governed by laws which can be discovered by the research scientist if only the right methods can be developed. The knowledge that is discovered using these methods is regarded as objective and factual, i.e. it is correct for all times and all places, and is not going to be different according to who discovers it. Once that knowledge is gained, it can be used to explain events in the natural world, to make predictions about what will happen in the natural world, and thus to control that world and make it behave in ways that are, at least in theory, to the advantage of the controllers. We will pursue this debate further in chapter 6 of this book, and find that this picture of natural science has been modified recently. For the moment, however, we will accept these assumptions.

The hypothetico-deductive method

This is the name given to the logic of the research method that natural science is thought to employ. It is illustrated in Figure 3.1. The process starts with the phenomena (1), out there in the world, which can be observed objectively. These sometimes casual observations prompt ideas in the mind of the

Figure 3.1 The hypothetico-deductive method

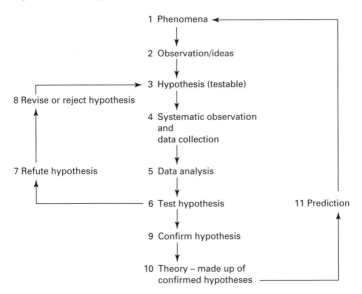

Source: McNeill and Townley 1986.

scientist (2), from which is developed an hypothesis (3). This is essentially an intelligent guess about what is happening, but in a form that can be tested. This test may be done as an experiment in the laboratory, or by further data collection 'in the field'. The scientist should try to prove the hypothesis wrong. This is because, however often an experiment comes out right, you can never be sure that it will come out right the next time, and so you can never be sure that your hypothesis is right. It only has to come out wrong once for you to know that the hypothesis is wrong. An experiment is then carried out (or data is collected in the field) (4), and the results are analysed (5). The hypothesis is then tested against these results (6). If the hypothesis is not supported by the evidence (7), it can be rejected or revised (8), and a fresh hypothesis developed (3). If it is supported by the evidence (9), then it can be seen as a contribution to theory (10). If the theory becomes elaborate enough, it begins to look like a law, and predictions about future events may be made (11).

Though experimental logic is in its most pure form in the laboratory, let us illustrate the method with an example from applied science. Suppose a scientist is trying to find out what will improve milk yield in cows. Ordinary observation will suggest to the researcher that things like the type of grass available, additions to diet, the amount of water drunk, and the frequency of milking all play their part. These factors will be taken one at a time and the scientist will set up experiments to test them. Being a scientist in a western society, the researcher is unlikely to think that music or magic have much influence.

The first hypothesis might be that 'milk yield is linked to the amounts of water cows drink and the intervals at which they drink it'. To test this, the experimenter must establish two groups of cows, the 'control group' and the 'experimental group'. Each group is matched in every possible way: species, age, health, etc. They will be put into identical environments which are controlled in every respect by the experimenter. The experimenter will then deliver a certain amount of water at regular intervals to the control group, but will systematically vary the amount of water delivered to the experimental group. If the milk yield of the experimental group varies, and the variation is linked to water intake, the experimenter is entitled to assume that there is a causal link between milk yield and water intake, since there is no other difference between the two groups. It would be a basic mistake to assume that the first correct answer is the only one that exists, so the scientist will conduct further experiments, trying all the time to prove the hypothesis wrong. If it cannot be proved wrong, then the scientist will conclude that there is a causal law in operation, and will advise farmers, who are likely to have paid for the research, of this.

The variable that is controlled by the experimenter is called the 'independent variable', and anything that varies as a result of this is called a 'dependent variable'. For example, the amount of fresh air for the cows might be the independent variable, and the milk yield would be the dependent variable.

To summarize: the purpose of the experiment is to create a standardized situation for the researcher to study, in which all variables are under the control of the experimenter, and in which the results of manipulating variables can be studied and measured. If some correlation is found between variables, the researcher has to show that this is a causal relationship rather than just a coincidence.

Laboratory experiments in social science

What relevance does this have for the social scientist? What aspects of human behaviour can be studied in the laboratory? What are the advantages of such an approach?

The laboratory method appeals to those who believe that, in the last analysis, human behaviour can be studied and explained in the same way as can events in the world of nature. There are assumed to be patterns of cause and effect that can be identified in regard to social behaviour and consequently, society. This, of course, is the positivist perspective discussed in Chapter 1. Experimentation as a social science method, as Moores (1998) notes 'can be seen as the essential positivist method' (p. 2) because it assumes that social scientists are the disinterested and objective pursuers of a truth that exists independent of society. The laboratory experiment, because of its emphasis on systematic, logical and controlled data collection, is seen as a process that minimizes subjectivity and keeps out the influence of the experimenter's own personal and political values. Moreover, the experiment is seen to offer a high level of reliability, i.e. other scientists can repeat the experiment to test out the findings and to check for flaws in the experimental design. Finally, the experiment offers the possibility of quantifying data in ways that assist the identification of patterns of social behaviour and correlations between social phenomena.

Despite the attraction of these positivist characteristics, the laboratory experiment has been used more by psychologists than sociologists, although many of the interests of the former overlap with the interests of sociology, especially in areas like media effects and the use of power. Milgram's experiment on the effects of authority on human behaviour is a good example of this. He set up an experiment, in laboratory conditions, where volunteers were instructed to teach and test a person who was in a separate room on a series of linked words and give them electric shocks every time the learner made a mistake. The shocks were to be increased with each error. What the 'teacher' volunteer did not know was that the whole experiment was an elaborate deception and that the 'learner' was in fact a co-worker of Milgram. No electric shocks were actually being transmitted. The experiment was actually concerned with how far people would obey others who held an official or expert position. Milgram found that twenty-six of his forty volunteers – 65 per cent – were prepared to administer the maximum shock to a stranger in these circumstances.

Another example of this type of research was reported by Haney *et al.* (1973). In this case, a simulated prison was created and twenty-four volunteers were randomly assigned to the roles of 'guard' or 'prisoner'. After instruction in the regulations of the 'prison' the volunteers were placed in it for nearly a week and their reactions and behaviour observed. The effects were dramatic. The experiment had to be ended early because of the behaviour it was inducing in both guards and prisoners. Many of the guards quickly showed that they enjoyed the power they had, and began to abuse it. Five prisoners had to be released because of extreme emotional depression and the rest seem relieved when the experiment ended. In contrast, nearly all of the guards expressed regret at having to finish the experiment early.

Experimental problems

Experiments on human beings are not without problems. For a start, human beings differ quite radically from the usual subjects of experiments. People uniquely have consciousness and consequently, self-awareness, unlike chemicals, atoms and even other animals. We have seen already that it is relatively easy to set up control and experimental groups in experiments using, say, animals, to introduce variables, to compare the two groups and conclude that the difference between the groups is caused by one particular independent variable. However, this approach may not be very effective with people. We may be able to gather together two groups of people with similar social characteristics, e.g. gender, age, ethnicity, education, even similar physical characteristics into control and experimental groups, but we cannot assume that differences between them are due to the variables we introduce into the experimental situation. As Sanders (1976) notes ' unlike natural scientists, however, sociologists deal with a subject matter that has a mind of its own, and they have therefore encountered problems not found in the natural sciences' (pp. 141–2). The fact is that it is impossible to find human control and experimental groups that are exactly alike because no two people are likely to share the same perception or interpretation of social reality. Our reaction to events may be dependent upon previous experience, emotional make-up, personality, etc. – factors which are both difficult to predict and control. It may not be the experimental conditions or treatment that is having the effect. Rather, it is the fact that the people who experienced one set of experimental conditions were already different from those who experienced another. In addition, as Gomm (2004) notes, 'the experimenter can't control what happened to a subject the previous night or on the bus on the way to the laboratory' (p. 30) and consequently the experimenter has little control over what happens to the research subject outside the laboratory which may also influence results.

These difficulties are compounded by the fact that the laboratory situation is an artificial environment and consequently there is likely to be a validity gap between people's behaviour in such situations and their behaviour in the real world. This may mean that people may behave different from usual if they know that an experiment is taking place, even if they do not fully understand what it is about. Sociologists have suggested that two distinct types of bias cause this deviation from normal or natural behaviour.

First, there may be an 'experimental effect' in which the bias is grounded in the subject's perception of the experiment. This effect, which is sometimes called the 'Hawthorne Effect' was first spotted in 1927 as being produced by an experiment devised by Professor Elton Mayo of Harvard University aimed at examining the relationship between working conditions, workers' tiredness and their productivity. He set up a test area in the Hawthorne Plant of the General Electric Company, where telephone relays were made. He used five female volunteers who knew the experiment was taking place. Working conditions were matched with those in the main work area, and Mayo then varied such things as room temperature, humidity, hours of work and rest-breaks. Observation in the first few months showed that, almost regardless of what changes were made, output went up, even when conditions were apparently worsened.

Five hypotheses were suggested to explain this, and each was tested. The most convincing turned out to be that the girls were responding to being involved in the experiment, and were developing strong group loyalties and a wish to please the experimenters. It was the fact of the experiment that was the important independent variable, not the ones that Mayo was working with.

Robson (2002) notes that experimental effect is bound up with what he calls the 'demand characteristics' of the experimental situation. This occurs because usually people who take part in experiments do not go into them free of expectation or with an open mind. They 'know that certain things are expected or demanded of them' (p. 112) and their resulting behaviour may consequently have little to do with the variables introduced by the experimenter. Instead, the resulting experimental data is likely to be the outcome of how the research subjects interpreted the situation into which the experimenter put them. For example, some research subjects may try to work out what is expected of them and respond accordingly whilst others may act in ways which they think shows them in a better light than others. Others are enthusiastic about the research because they have an interest in it and would prefer the results to come out in a certain way – consider, for example, how male and female experimental subjects might react to an experiment on gender differences. Rosnow and Rosenthal (1997) note that people who volunteer for experiments are more likely to have these sorts of biases than those who have been press-ganged. The only way to avoid these problems is for the researcher to deceive those who take part in the experiment by telling them that it is about one thing when it is really about another. However, some sociologists would prefer to avoid deceit on ethical grounds.

A second potential source of bias may result from 'experimenter expectancy effect'. Rosnow and Rosenthal note that, often unwittingly, the beliefs, values and expectations of the experimenter can affect every stage of the research process so that findings fit what the experimenters expected to happen.

Such bias, whether conscious or unconscious, will undermine the validity of data gathered by the experiment. Robson notes that some experimenters have attempted to avoid this problem by minimizing contact between the experimental team and research subjects, although this strategy increases the artificial nature of the experiment (and consequently leaves the research data open to the criticism that it is the product of artificial rather than natural behaviour). Some experimenters have contracted-out data collection so that people working directly with the research subjects do not know what hypothesis is being tested and consequently are unlikely to pass biases on.

Gomm identifies fraud as a further type of expectancy effect and suggests that it is fairly common in scientific research. Some of this is deliberate but much is the result of self-delusion. Expecting to achieve a particular type of data can result in biased observation, interpretation and recording. For example, a researcher might interpret data which is unexpected as 'errors' or 'false starts' and not record it thus biasing the results in a particular direction. If results are ambiguous and difficult to interpret, researchers might apply 'benefit of doubt' in a way that supports their hypothesis.

Some sociologists have questioned what is called the 'external validity' of the controlled experiment. This refers to the fact that even the most well-designed and controlled experiment is 'usually a gross over-simplification of what happens under real-life circumstances. This means that experimental results may not be very enlightening as to what actually happens in the real world' (Gomm 2004: 22). In other words, experiments are artificial and at best they only tell us what happens to people under experimental conditions. It was for this reason that Baldwin and McConville (1979) chose to study real juries rather than follow the example of previous researchers in setting up 'mock trials'. However, Gomm argues that this criticism is unfair because he argues that it is not the point of experiments 'to match real life point by point' (p. 43). Experiments focus on 'interesting bits of reality' and allow the experimenter to isolate interesting factors which might be lost in the multitude of possible real-life influences. The data collected in the experimental situation can, then, be followed-up and possibly verified by studying more realistic situations.

There are ethical constraints governing the use of experiments in sociology too. Particular types of research are always going to be problematic. For example, it would be clearly wrong to deprive very young children of any contact with parents or adults to assess the impact of socialization or to expose them to violent videos for a long period of time to see whether this has any negative effects upon their behaviour.

Finally, experiments have been criticized by some for their lack of representativeness. Experiments tend to be expensive and consequently, the sample size used tends to be small. This makes it difficult to generalize from experimental data to the wider population. This is complicated further by the social characteristics of experimental samples which are often not representative of the wider population. For example, as Gomm points out, co-operative people are over-represented and unco-operative people under-represented. Suls and Rostow (1988) also note that university students are greatly over-represented in psychology experiments.

Field experiments

Partly in response to such criticisms, some researchers have conducted 'field experiments'. These take place in the real world and those involved do not know that an experiment is being conducted. Such experiments tend to relax experimental controls to produce more naturalistic conditions. Field experiments also appeal to interpretivist sociologists because they tend to focus on how the real world is interpreted by the people who inhabit it. Field experiments tend to focus on interaction between individuals, and to an extent, allow us to explore the meanings attached by people to a range of social situations and social relationships. In particular, field experiments have given us insight into social processes such as labelling, stereotyping and discrimination.

The most well-known sociological field experiment is that carried out by Rosenthal and Jacobson – 'Pygmalion in the Classroom'. In this 1968 experiment, the researchers told teachers that 20 per cent of their new intake had scored very highly on an intelligence test. In reality, the 20 per cent of pupils had been selected at random. Over a period of eighteen months, the researchers found that the 20 per cent sample had made significant improvements in their school work compared with the other 80 per cent of the new intake. Rosenthal and Jacobson concluded that this progress was due to a 'self-fulfilling prophecy' – the teachers had responded more positively to these children in the classroom and some-how communicated the label of 'high achievers' to the children who had responded to the attention given to them.

Another key field experiment is the 'pseudo-patient' experiment conducted by David Rosenhan (1973) which involved members of his team presenting themselves as voluntary patients into various American mental hospitals, complaining that they were hearing voices. Each was admitted as suffering from schizophrenic symptoms. Once admitted, they were instructed by Rosenhan to behave as sanely as possible and to record their interactions with medical staff. None of the 'pseudo-patients' were caught out or discharged as cured. Instead, after varying lengths of time, they were discharged as being 'in remission', i.e. their schizophrenia was thought to be still present, but not actually revealing itself in their behaviour. Rosenhan concludes that the treatment of mental illness has more to do with the labels that are attached to the illness by medical staff than the symptoms exhibited by the patient. For example, one pseudo-patient who took notes on how he was treated in the hospital was described by staff as exhibit-ing 'writing behaviour' – in other words, perfectly normal behaviour was interpreted by doctors as abnormal and as a symptom of mental illness. Some commentators, notably Gomm (2004) have questioned whether Rosenhan's research is truly an experiment because he did not use any form of control group – Gomm argues Rosenhan's work is really a form of covert participant observation.

The work of Smith (1977) is a good example of a true field experiment. Smith was interested in the extent of racial disadvantage in Britain and set up an experiment in which actors from a range of ethnic backgrounds but with identical CVs applied for a range of real jobs and covertly recorded their interaction with the mainly white employers. This experiment, which was repeated by Brown and Gay (1985) and the television programme 'Black and White' in the late 1990s, indicated that racial discrimination was still very influential in creating inequalities in employment.

A variation on the field experiment is what Gomm calls the 'decision-simulation' experiment. These are normally focused on situations in which people reading and writing documents and making decisions is a normal and natural process. The best known example of this type of experiment is that of Atkinson *et al.* (1975) which investigated how British and Danish coroners differed in their approach to investigating suicide.

Having noted that the suicide rate is markedly higher in Denmark than in England, Atkinson and his colleagues hypothesized that this might be the result of different procedures for certifying deaths as suicides. Five Danish medical officers and four English coroners were supplied with details of forty cases of sudden death, half English and half Danish, and were asked to give a verdict of suicide, accident, homicide, natural causes, or 'open'. On average, the English coroners decided on a suicide verdict for nineteen of the cases, whereas the Danes averaged twenty-nine suicide verdicts. Even allowing for the artificiality of the situation and for the small number of participants, this suggests that the hypothesis was supported.

Another example of a decision-simulation experiment was that conducted by Owusu-Bempah (1994) who investigated social workers' decisions about children to see whether any differences could be discerned in their treatment of black and white children. They presented a set of case notes to social workers which were extremely similar in content in regard to the history of the children but which occasionally highlighted their ethnic background. The results showed clearly that social workers responded to the fact of the children's ethnicity and interpreted their needs quite differently.

Gomm argues that in such simulation experiments, it needs to be remembered that there may be some bias because the subjects know that the decision-making process is not real and consequently their experimental behaviour may not accord with their natural behaviour. However, Gomm notes that the difference between reality and the experimental conditions is likely to be minimal in decision-simulation experiments because this sort of decision-making is usually subjected to public scrutiny anyway and such officials will, therefore, be used to being observed and having to account to someone for their actions.

Field experiments are attractive because it is seen as easier to generalize results to the real world if experiments are conducted in a natural setting. As we saw earlier, there is also a tendency for laboratory volunteers to be unrepresentative of the general population. Field experiments are less vulnerable to the experimenter-effect problems generated by demand characteristics. As Robson (2002) notes 'real tasks in a real world setting are less prone to . . . game playing, so you are more likely to be measuring what you think you are measuring' (p. 115). However, field experiments have other problems of their own. As Robson notes, 'moving outside the safe confines of the laboratory may well be traumatic' (p. 113). The major one is that there is no way that the researcher can hope to be aware of, still less control, all the possible independent variables, and this casts doubt on any conclusions that may be drawn about causes.

The problem works both ways. If we are to control all variables, we have to set up a totally artificial situation. If we want the situation to be as realistic as possible, we have to accept that we cannot control all the variables, and can therefore never be sure that the cause and effect relationships we identify are, in fact, correct.

There are also ethical problems with field experiments. Rosenthal and Jacobson's research has particularly been criticized because it may have damaged the educational progress of the other 80 per cent of the school's new intake who perhaps did not receive the same quality of teacher attention. They have also been criticized for misleading the teachers. Moreover, Rosenthal and Jacobson assume a causal link between teacher behaviour and improved attainment but everyday interaction between teachers and pupils was not subjected to intensive observation and data collection. Therefore, at best, their conclusions are speculative.

Clearly, then, most field experiments present ethical problems for the researcher because they involve manipulation of behaviour and deception. However, some sociologists believe that these ethical problems are worth living with because if we do seek 'informed consent', we may actually lose some of the advantages of moving outside the laboratory.

In conclusion, then, field experiments, for all their faults, 'represent a tremendously effective way of "getting inside" group behaviour, generating interesting qualitative data in a naturally occurring context and allowing interpretive sociologists to get close to their subject matter' (Moores 1998: 4).

Ethnomethodology

This very specialized approach is explained on pp. 128–30, but it is mentioned here because it sometimes uses a kind of experiment. The experiments are of the 'what if' variety, i.e. they ask 'what would happen if we did this?', and are not therefore based on hypothetico-deductive logic.

Garfinkel, the most high-profile ethnomethodologist, was particularly interested in the commonsense rules that govern everyday interaction. He argued that the best way to uncover these rules was to break them and he devised a number of 'breaching' or 'disrupting' experiments in order to do this. For example, he asked his students to spend short periods at home acting like formal lodgers rather than sons or daughters. For example, the students asked permission of their parents to engage in certain types of behaviour and volunteered themselves for household tasks. As their sons and daughters became more polite and detached, parents became confused, frustrated and angry because 'normal' interaction that was usually characterized by informality, casual rudeness and friendly intimacy had broken down. Garfinkel's students were accused by family members of being inconsiderate, selfish and even mentally ill. Social order was only restored when the experiment was explained to parents.

The British anthropologist, Kate Fox (2004), has recently conducted similar experiments into rule-breaking in order to understand the hidden rules of English behaviour. She deliberately flouted rules in regard to bumping into people in the street, asking people the price of their house and queue-jumping in order to gain insight into English reserve and courtesy. For example, she noted as part of her bumping experiment that:

> I tried to make my experiments as scientific as possible by bumping into a representative cross-section of the English population, in a representative sample of locations. Somewhat to my surprise . . . about 80% of my victims said 'sorry' when I lurched into them, even though the collisions were clearly my fault . . . by way of 'controls', I diligently bumped into as many people as I could in France, Belgium, Italy, Russia, Poland and Lebanon. Recognising that this would not constitute a representative international sample, I also bumped into tourists of different nationalities at tourist-trap locations in London and Oxford. Only the Japanese (surprise, surprise) seemed to have anything even approaching the English sorry-reflex.

> (Fox 2004: 148–9)

Comparison and the comparative method

Experiments involve comparing what happens in one situation (the control group) with what happens in another (the experimental group). Though it is clear that the true experiment is of limited use in sociology, it is important to recognize the central role that comparison plays in all social scientific explanation.

There is, for example, the 'natural experiment' or 'quasi-experiment' ('quasi' means 'as if'). This is done when some identifiable change takes place, perhaps in the law or in social policy, and the researcher studies its effects by comparing the before-and-after situation or the situation in a group where the change has taken place with one where it has not. Comparison is also used to explain a current phenomenon by comparing the past experience of the group where it is occurring with that of a group where it is not occurring. In public health, this was the method used to establish that cigarette-smoking is a major cause of lung cancer, and it was also the key technique used to identify some of the factors involved in the spread of HIV infection. For example, it showed that it was not the injecting of illegal drugs that caused HIV infection but the using of shared and dirty needles (Aggleton 1990). Aggleton calls this the 'retrospective experiment'. Instead of setting up situations either in the laboratory or in the field, the researcher studies what is already going on. The method of argument is based on the same underlying logic as the experiment. It is worth noting, in passing, that many natural sciences also have to rely solely on observation and comparison, for example, astronomy, seismology and climatology.

Comparison can also be important when the researcher is trying to establish what is *not* an independent variable. Thus, Barker (1984), in her study of the Moonies, gave a questionnaire similar to that which she had given to the Moonies to a group of people who were matched with the Moonies with respect to sex, age and background. Only when she had this data could she say with any confidence whether people who were converted into their church, the Unification Church (the dependent variable), were different in any systematic ways from the rest of the population.

Comparison was extensively used as *the* method of analysis and explanation (the comparative method) by many early sociologists when trying to identify the major historical patterns of social change. Weber and Durkheim, in particular, based their work firmly on the comparative method. Weber was interested in the reasons for the emergence of capitalism in Western Europe. Why did it occur when it did? Other societies had had similar social and economic systems to that of Europe and had not developed capitalism. Weber studied, particularly, China and India, but also ancient Palestine and some Islamic countries. Despite their similarities, only Europe had developed capitalism. What Weber sought was a factor that was unique to Europe that he could show was logically connected with the emergence of capitalism.

He found it in Protestantism, or at least the Calvinist version of it. Calvinists believed that every person was predestined by God to go to heaven or to hell. Nothing they could do on earth would affect this destiny. However, rather than seeing this as an excuse for living as they pleased, the Calvinists believed that success in work and in trade was a sign that they were one of the elect rather than one of the damned. Needing this reassurance, they were thus encouraged to innovate, to work hard and to strive to succeed. However, if their efforts were crowned with success in the form of wealth, they could not spend this profit on worldly goods and comforts, since their religion forbade this. Instead, they would reinvest it in their business enterprises, which would then flourish even more. It is this principle of reinvestment and growth that is the basis of capitalism.

Thus Weber claimed to show that Calvinism was the independent variable that was present in Europe and absent in China and India, and was one of the important causes of the appearance of the dependent variable of capitalism. In addition to showing simply that the factors occurred together, Weber was also able to show that there was an understandable connection between the Calvinists' beliefs and their actions. We can imagine that, if we believed what the Calvinists believed, we would have behaved in the same way.

For Durkheim, comparison was the most important method of sociological analysis: 'Comparative sociology is not a branch of sociology. It is sociology itself' (Durkheim 1895). He used it in a number of studies but his most famous example of comparative method was his study of the causes of suicide (Durkheim 1897). In doing this research, Durkheim collected the statistics of suicide in the various areas and regions of France, and of other European countries. He calculated these as suicide rates in relation to the size of the population in which they occurred. Having considered and dismissed various other explanations of suicide, Durkheim then showed how these rates varied systematically with the rates of various other social phenomena, such as religious belief, marital status, urban or rural living and military training or the lack of it. With the help of a mass of statistical calculations, all presented in his book, he showed that there were correlations between these different rates, but he had yet to show that these correlations were causal connections and not mere coincidence. This he did by using the concept of 'social integration'. By manipulating the statistics in various ways, holding one factor constant while varying another, he showed that rates of suicide varied according to the extent to which people were integrated into their social group. Over-integration or under-integration could both cause suicide, as could the disintegration of the group itself, leaving the individual rootless and without moral and social support.

More recently, the comparative method has emerged as the major method of analysis in the sociology of development which is concerned with fundamental questions about the relationship between the developed and developing worlds. Progress or lack of it in the developing world is measured by comparing a range of data relating to mortality, life expectancy, health care, literacy, etc. with that experienced in the developed world. For example, Erikson and Goldthorpe (1993) used the comparative method in their international study of social mobility. They used data taken from twelve national studies conducted between 1970 and 1978, and recoded data about occupational and, therefore, social class backgrounds, using a new set of categories. They particularly focused on comparing Western European countries with Eastern Europe countries which had recently experienced the collapse of communism. To their surprise, they found few differences in opportunities for upward social mobility across these regions.

The comparative method is often used in studies of educational achievement. Jesson *et al.* (1992) investigated what difference attending one school rather than another can make to the educational achievement of similar children. They compared seventy-four schools in Nottinghamshire in 1991 taking into consideration such factors as gender, social class, poverty (as measured by the percentage of pupils receiving free school meals) and the ethnic mix of schools. Wiliam and Bartholomew (2004) analysed the results of 995 teenagers in six London schools, comparing their GCSE maths grades in 2000 with their 1998 key stage 3 scores. They found dramatic differences in progress made by pupils of similar ability according to the set in which they are placed. For example, secondary pupils placed in mathematics top sets scored up to three grades higher at GCSE than they would have done if placed in the bottom set.

Finally, longitudinal surveys and cohort studies also involve comparative analysis, and as such, can be seen as types of natural experiment. Longitudinal surveys are explored in greater detail on pp. 53–5 and involve comparing samples throughout an extended period of time. For example, the national birth surveys have followed samples of children born in a particular week in 1946 (over 5,000 children), 1958 (17,000 children) and 1970 (16,000 children) and compared their outcomes in regard to factors such as delinquency, health and educational achievement.

Cohort studies, in contrast, tend to compare the performance of more specific groups over a period of time in a specific context such as a school. Smith and Tomlinson (1989), for example, collected data about the same cohort of 3,000 pupils spread across twenty multicultural inner city comprehensive schools, following them from their entry into secondary school to their GCSE examinations. Marmot (1995) tracked 17,000 male civil servants throughout their careers and, in many cases, into retirement over a period of twenty-five years. He compared their specific jobs, i.e. managerial, white collar and manual workers, with time taken off work for stress, types of illness and mortality rates. He was able to conclude that the lower the occupational status within the civil service, the more likely the worker was to experience high levels of stress, chronic, long-term illness and premature death. Moreover, Marmot's comparative analysis clearly showed that health inequalities between high-status and low-status civil servants were actually increasing.

The comparative method, then, has proved itself to be highly sustainable as a sociological research tool over the past one hundred years. As we can see, it still remains very much in use. However, this is not to say that it is problem free. Doubts have been expressed about comparative studies which use official statistics because of the suspicion that such data is socially constructed (see p. 138). There is also the problem of how the comparative units are defined and operationalized. For example, sociologists working with comparative analysis in the field of development studies are not in agreement as to what constitutes 'development' and 'progress'. Neo-modernization theorists see development as adopting western institutions and ideas, whereas more radical thinkers see development as economic and social well-being which is achieved within a context of autonomy and liberation from Western influences. The existence of these competing ideologies working within the same field means that comparative analysis may depend on interpretations that other sociologists may reject.

4

Ethnography

'Ethnography' literally means writing about the way of life, or culture, of social groups. At its simplest, it involves the researcher inserting themselves into the natural setting of the social group being studied and participating in and observing their daily activities. Other methods, particularly informal interviews and the analysis of documents such as diaries may be used to sketch out a fuller picture.

The purpose of such research is to describe the culture and life style of the group of people being studied in a way that is as faithful as possible to the way they see it themselves and to the social contexts in which their behaviour occurs. The idea is not so much to seek causes and explanations, as is often the case with survey-style research, but rather to 'tell it like it is', to capture what Brewer (2000) notes are 'social meanings and ordinary activities' (p. 6).

The aims of ethnographic research are strongly linked to the broader theoretical frameworks of phenomenology and interpretivism (see pp. 15–21) which argue that all social action is intentional. In other words, people choose to behave the way they do. Interpretivist sociologists argue that in order to understand social life, we must first examine social interaction and especially the social meanings or interpretations that people attach to their behaviour. They argue that we can only do this by adopting ethnographic research methods because these allow researchers access to the 'lived experience' of particular social groups and to think themselves into the perspectives of their members. Ethnography, therefore, is about imitating real life. Weber called this 'verstehen', i.e. being able to emphathize with or think like the people that are being studied. This closeness to the research subjects has led interpretivists to claim that ethnography produces the most valid and authentic type of qualitative data of any type of social research method.

The history of ethnography

The origins of modern ethnography are to be found in the work of the classical social anthropologists such as D.T. Evans-Pritchard, Bronislaw Malinowski, A.R. Radcliffe-Brown and the American Margaret Mead. These anthropologists generally adopted what Tedlock (2000) calls the 'sympathetic method' which involved gaining the trust of the natives that were being studied by sympathizing and participating in their way of life. Malinowski is usually regarded as the greatest of these researchers, at least as far as his methods are concerned. In order to see things as the Trobriand Islanders saw them, he joined their communities, learned their language and lived among them as a member, noting and recording his observations in preparation for writing about them later. Mead, too, went to live among the New Guinea tribes she was studying, observed their behaviour as a participant in the society, and combined this with some informal interviewing of members of the tribes.

From about the 1930s onwards, sociology and anthropology grew apart as sociologists concentrated their attention on

complex industrial societies and anthropologists continued
to study simple societies. Recently, there has been a moving
together again, but in the 1930s there developed at the
University of Chicago a tradition of social research that is
now known as the 'Chicago School'. Led by Robert E. Park,
this group of researchers, as we saw in Chapter 1, devoted
their research efforts to detailed studies of their own city. Park
specifically recommended that his team followed the methods
pioneered by the anthropologists:

> Go and sit in the lounges of the luxury hotels and on the
> doorsteps of the flophouses; sit on the Gold Coast settees
> and on the slum shakedowns; sit in Orchestra Hall and
> in the Star and Garter Burlesk. In short, gentlemen, go get
> the seats of your pants dirty in *real* research.
>
> (Park, quoted in Gomm and McNeill 1982)

The Chicago School employed ethnographic methods
of data collection and produced accounts of the lives of a wide
variety of social groups, with an emphasis on the poor and the
deviant. They concentrated on observation of people in their
'natural habitat', watching, listening, talking, putting together
life-histories and recording.

The pupils of this generation of sociologists were people
like Howard Becker and Erving Goffman, and it was their
pioneering work in the 1960s that gave a new lease of life to
ethnographic research after it had fallen into some disuse,
in British sociology at least, in the 1950s. The period between
1967 and 1980 was particularly fertile for ethnographic
research, especially in the fields of education and deviance,
and the data collected led to new insights into power relationships in the classroom, the interaction between police officers
and suspects on the beat, and why some social activities,
particularly those associated with youth cultures, were defined
as a social problem by society. Ethnographic research in
this period was responsible for improving our knowledge
and understanding of concepts and social processes such as

stereotyping, labelling, the self-fulfilling prophecy and sub-cultures. Feminists, too, actively engaged in this type of research in this period, particularly in the field of education, and the findings of their observational studies were instrumental in the development of more girl-friendly teaching and learning strategies introduced into schools in the late 1980s.

The role of observation in ethnographic research

The main purpose of ethnographic research is to understand the social meanings and activities of people as they go about their everyday social life. A range of research techniques, including in-depth interviewing and analysis of personal documents have been used to get close to research subjects, but the ethnographic technique which has proved to be the most effective is generally thought to be 'observation'. Robson (2002) notes that there are three broad ways in which observation has been used in sociological research; 'direct or non-participant observation', which was particularly popular as a method for studying educational contexts such as classrooms in the 1960s and 1970s; 'participant observation', which has always been the central method of ethnographers; and 'complete' or 'covert' observation.

Direct or non-participant observation

Some ethnographic research involves the use of direct or non-participant observation. The sociologist who uses this technique takes on the role of a detached onlooker who carries out detailed analyses of social activity. Usually, this unobtrusive form of observation will be structured in that it will use a coded observation schedule which will operationalize aspects of the research question or hypothesis and direct what is to be observed. The observation is therefore focused on particular types of behaviour or activity; activity that does not fit the schedule is ignored. This type of structure is especially appealing to those sociologists who stress the need for scientific method because it produces 'facts' in the form of quantifiable data.

This type of observation has been mainly used in two contexts. First, it is often used in experimental situations. Subjects may be watched through one-way glass or by using audio and visual technology. Second, it was used extensively between the 1960s and 1980s in a field context. In particular, many educational sociologists found themselves in classrooms, playing a non-participatory role observing the content and process of lessons, interactions between teachers and pupils, the effectiveness of teaching and learning and pupil peer cultures.

Most of these sociologists used observation schedules based on interaction-process analysis, a method of coding which attempted to classify behaviour in groups into particular categories. For example, Flanders (1970) devised ten categories of teacher/student behaviour which many observers adopted for categorizing and recording classroom activities. The observer's task is then to observe what goes on in a classroom and, every three seconds, to tick the category that best describes what has been happening during that period. This produces a statistical, or 'quantified', account of what is going on, which can then be compared with other lessons and other teachers. An interesting variation on this technique was Barton *et al.*'s (1980) five-category observation schedule for their study of interaction between staff and residents in a home for the elderly (see Box 4.1). Other observers have used 'interaction charts' based on seating plans which maps specific lines of communication between individuals by the use of arrows. Ticks next to particular names indicate that the individual addressed the whole group.

The main reason for using unobtrusive observation is to minimize or eliminate the risk that people will be affected by the presence of a new member of their social group. However, unobtrusive observation in a field context involves the observer being visibly present and consequently, even if the researcher is not participating, there is still the likelihood that his or

---

Box 4.1 Categories for naturally occurring interactions between staff and residents in a home for the elderly

1 Independent behaviour – a resident's carrying out of bathing, dressing, grooming or toileting tasks without assistance
2 Dependent behaviour – a resident's request for, or acceptance of, assistance in bathing, etc.
3 Independence-supportive behaviour – verbal encouragement of resident independence from staff or staff discouragement of, or scolding for, resident's requests for assistance
4 Dependence-supportive behaviour – staff assistance in a resident's personal maintenance, praise for an resident's acceptance of help and staff discouragement of independent behaviour
5 Other behaviour – staff or resident behaviour that is not related to personal maintenance tasks.

(Barton *et al.*, quoted in C. Robson 2002)

---

her presence is affecting what is happening. For example, pupil behaviour may be shaped by their curiosity about the researcher's motives whilst teachers may feel threatened or compromised by another adult's presence in their classroom. It has also been suggested that objectivity can be difficult to achieve because observers have to make value judgements about whether behaviour or activities fit particular categories on their observation schedule. Other researchers may disagree with the interpretation of what counts as a significant event which raises the issue of how reliable such recording is.

Participant observation

'Participant observation' is the main method used by ethnographers. It can be distinguished from the quantitative research methods discussed in Chapter 2 because it is research driven from the 'inside' rather than research imposed from the 'outside'. Research methods such as questionnaires and interviews involve the sociologist as the 'outsider looking in' and consequently, as we have already seen, run the risk of imposing the sociologist's own values and interpretations on those being studied. Participant observation, on the other hand, involves the sociologist being on the inside because he or she joins in with the activities of those being studied and shares their experiences of social reality. Interpretations of behaviour, therefore, are based on watching, observing, listening and probing by talking to those being researched so that the data authentically reflects the vantage point of the participants themselves.

Participant observation takes a great deal of skill if it is to be carried out effectively. The ability to establish a trusting rapport with people in the group being studied is crucial. Observation also requires patience and a clear focus. A great deal of time is spent 'hanging around' and the researcher needs to be trained in heightened watching and listening skills in order to spot the significant events which may evolve naturally and slowly out of what seem like trivial activities and interactions. The pace of the group must not be forced by the observer's impatience that nothing seems to be going on. Furthermore, the participant observer needs to be able to skilfully engage in informal interviewing that naturally flows from the social situations in which the group and researcher find themselves. The observer also needs to make decisions about how what is observed is going to be recorded. For example, should the observer attempt to structure and quantify the observational data? Should it be presented in narrative form so that those observed speak for themselves? As we shall see later, the question 'what should be selected from the mass of observation data recorded for final analysis?' has proved a methodological thorn-in-the-side for most participant observers.

The role of the participant observer

An important decision for those planning to use participant observation concerns the role that is going to be adopted in terms of the extent of the participation in the life of the group being studied. The researcher might decide to be a 'complete participant' and hide their true identity and motives from the group. This covert form of observation requires the researcher to be skilled at acting out a credible role so that the suspicion of the infiltrated group is not raised. On the other hand, the sociologist may choose the role of 'participant as observer' in which the sociological motives and goals of the observer are made clear to the group or, at least, key members of it from the very beginning. The researcher will endeavour to take part in the daily activities of the group. Most participant-as-observer researchers acknowledge that the early behaviour of the group is likely to be artificial as they respond to the researcher's presence. The hope is that the group eventually takes his or her presence for granted so that their behaviour can return to 'normal'. Some sociologists note that if the participant-as-observer role is to be successful, the researcher must maintain a delicate balance between being an insider, i.e. getting close to the subjects and establishing a rapport, and being an outsider, i.e. adopting the professional role of detached observer who can avoid getting too emotionally involved with the group.

Brewer points out that participant observation has been used in a variety of ways. Most observers are interested in understanding the world from the point of view of those being studied. However, ethnomethodologists such as Garfinkel (see pp. 128–30) have used observation as part of a series of spontaneous experiments aimed at disrupting the rules that govern routine everyday activities.

Most participant-observation research involves observers participating in fields and taking on roles with which they are unfamiliar. Other sociologists will send observers into situations with which they are familiar. For example, Rosenhan

(1973) was a doctor who became a patient in order to observe how mental illness was interpreted by medical staff. Other types of observation make use of a role that the researcher already occupies. This is known as 'observant participation'. Holdaway's (1983) study of police culture in a Sheffield police station is a good example of this. Holdaway was a police sergeant who conducted covert observation of his fellow officers as part of his research for his part-time sociology degree.

Whatever strategy is adopted, participant observation is very laborious and time-consuming, involving the researcher full-time for at least a matter of months, and sometimes years. It is expensive in terms of paying the salary or the research grant of the researcher for this time, especially if he or she is engaged in no other work.

The theoretical debate

As we saw in Chapter 1, two models of social research have dominated debate about how sociologists should go about studying the world; the natural science model based on positivism, and the anti-positivist model of interpretivism focused on uncovering the social meanings that underpin social action.

The positivist critique

Positivist analyses of ethnographic methods are generally not very complimentary. In fact, they suggest that participant observation is often the epitome of 'bad' science, and that its design and analysis breaches fundamental rules of scientific procedure. First, much participant observation is unsystematic and unstructured because it focuses on naturally occurring behaviour. Positivists despair of the fact that observers make no attempt to control possible influential variables. Second, positivist research stresses objectivity, the researcher as the disinterested pursuer of scientific truth. However, participant observation requires the researcher to be part of the study and consequently, there is always the possibility that their presence may become obtrusive and influence the behaviour that is being observed. Third, it is not possible to judge from ethnographic research whether the social context or the people studied are in any way typical, or representative. Fourth, positivists object strongly to the fact that observational data is difficult to replicate and, therefore, verify because much of it is the product of the unique relationship the researcher has built up with members of the group. It is extremely likely that another sociologist, even with similar social character-istics, would have a qualitatively different relationship with the group and consequently produce quite different sets of data. Reliability, then, cannot be guaranteed.

Positivists also object to the nature of the data collected by observational methods. Positivists prefer to see evidence of phenomena expressed in quantitative form because of the ease with which comparisons can be made. Some observation studies do use schedules which can produce statistical data, but most do not. Many ethnographic studies prefer to let their subjects speak for themselves, and observational evidence is often expressed in a qualitative form, e.g. long quotations, extracts from conversations, field notes, etc. which are not quantifiable and can be difficult to compare with each other or with other evidence. Therefore, positivists claim this type of data is too subjective.

Observational data is seen as unscientific because it is seen to be the result of the researcher's selective interpretations, i.e. the researcher has experienced thousands of social inter-actions, but in practice only a few can be selected for analysis and publication. Positivists are consequently very keen to question the representativeness of this type of qualitative evidence, i.e. how representative are the descriptions of what went on most of the time? Moreover, they are sceptical, too, about the validity of the data, i.e. they suggest that behaviour which does not fit the researcher's perspective is likely to be ignored or to be given less priority and attention at the analysis stage. Ethnography is also criticized because it necessarily involves a narrow view of the group or institution studied because the researcher cannot, by definition, study the wider context within which the research setting is located.

These criticisms have stung some ethnographers into developing scientific procedural rules especially in regard to reliability. For example, in addition to observation schedules, some studies have used two or more observers in order to verify what is being observed. Unfortunately, this inter-observer verification is really only suitable for very structured forms of observation such as non-participant observation.

The anti-positivist position

Interpretive sociology takes an anti-positivist position and stresses the need to investigate subjective experience. Consequently, it strongly recommends the use of ethnographic methods because they allow researchers to access the intimate and creative world of social meanings and action. It is the researcher's task to 'get inside the heads' of their subjects until it is possible to see their world as they do. This cannot be achieved through a structured interview or a questionnaire. Theories and explanations must emerge from the work as it goes along.

Participant observation appeals to interpretivist sociologists because of its 'naturalistic' qualities. The qualitative account produced by observational research is rooted in the natural setting of what is being described, and is thus very different from both the formal interview and laboratory research, which involve creating an artificial situation in which the data is collected. David Matza, for example, argues that the positivist focus on the exclusive use of questionnaires and formal interviews means that the young delinquent is never studied in his own natural setting, where his behaviour is natural and unself-conscious. Responses to an interview conducted by a stranger, however relaxed and friendly, can never provide a valid picture of the way of life of the subject of the interview.

The postmodernist position

Postmodernism rejects the claims made by both the natural science and the naturalistic interpretivist models of social research. Postmodernists reject the positivist view that there exists a 'reality' or 'truth' that can be captured by scientific research methods. From a postmodernist perspective, there are many 'realities' and 'truths' – all knowledge is selective and relative. Moreover, all accounts of research, including ethnography and the 'knowledge' that results from it, are a social construction in that the end result of research is only one researcher's interpretation of that evidence. Ethnographic descriptions are essentially autobiographical in that they only tell us how that particular ethnographer constructed their version of what went on around them. Postmodernists do not see such research as an authoritative insider-view of the social world. Rather it is merely one story because social life is made up of multiple realities, all of which have equal validity. Postmodernists therefore conclude that ethnographers should not claim that their research is an accurate representation of reality. Rather they argue that the ethnographic focus should be on 'reflexivity', i.e. 'stories from the field' that show the social processes, and especially the actions of the researcher, that impinge upon and contribute to the 'construction' of data.

The question of ethics

Observation studies have raised several ethical issues as a choice of research method. Brewer notes that ethnographers are more or less unique among researchers because they share in the lives of the people they study – 'they pry into people's innermost secrets, witness their failures and participate in their lives' (2000: 89). It is therefore important that observers adopt some sort of ethical code that respects their subjects. The guidelines laid down by the British Sociological Association's statement of ethics which can be found on the internet at http://www.britsoc.org.uk are what most sociologists in the UK follow.

The BSA code stresses the need to obtain informed consent, the need to protect the privacy and identity of individuals and the need to avoid inflicting physical, social and emotional harm. These issues are generally discussed on pp. 12–14, but some matters specific to participant observation are worth discussing further here. The BSA is especially concerned with the use of covert methods which are most frequently used by ethnographers. The BSA code clearly states that there are 'ethical dangers' in using such methods, namely that such methods violate the principles of informed consent and invade the privacy of those being studied. The BSA advises that covert methods should only be used if no other methods are suitable and if the data required is essential. If possible, consent for publication should be obtained from the group being studied after the research has been carried out.

The BSA code is also supported by the fact that most researchers start from the assumption that it is morally wrong to conduct research on people who do not know that they are being studied, and will therefore tell them at least that they are writing a book, even if they are not wholly frank about what the book is going to be about. Burgess (1984) argues that sociological researchers should always tell the truth except under very special circumstances such as maintaining confidentiality or protecting the identity of other sources. Bosk (1979) makes his view very clear: 'The privilege of being an observer is a gift presented to the researcher by his host and subjects.' Consequently, Bosk believes that sociologists need to be open about their motives – people, and specifically, friendships should not be used as a sociological resource, otherwise the relationship between researcher and subjects becomes abusive. Holdaway (1983) admits that documenting the work of police colleagues and friends made him feel uncomfortable.

Some qualitative researchers have suggested that informed consent may not always be feasible. Lawton (2002) who used observation in her study of dying patients at a hospice suggests that many of her patients were not alert enough to fully understand the aims and consequences of her research. On the other hand, Fine and Sandstrom (1988) argue that while consent for children to take part in research needs to be obtained from parents, young children should be given as much information as possible about the research and researcher. This would allow them to judge whether they want to take part in the research or not.

Despite these ethical concerns, some researchers have continued to emphasize the merits of covert observation. Those who argue in its favour point out that some groups will always be closed to research because the group is criminal, deviant, hostile to research or powerful enough to say no to researchers. For example, Fielding (1981) justified his use of covert observation of the National Front on the grounds that this racist organization would reject any overt research advances. Fielding actually joined the party and participated in meetings, organized demonstrations and marched in public. Similarly, Brewer (1984) joined the extreme right-wing Action Party in order to access former fascists. Calvey's (2000) study of bouncers, Winlow's (2000) study of the everyday world of violent men, *Badfellas*, and Armstrong's (1998) study of football hooliganism, all used covert observation, because they believed that the 'deviant' activities of these groups would not be revealed using either quantitative methods or even overt forms of observation.

Another strong argument in favour of covert research is the fact that a group's behaviour is likely to be disrupted by the presence of a known researcher. A proficient covert researcher who successfully acts a role is less likely to disturb the natural setting and more likely to mine a rich vein of authentic behaviour. Some researchers also suggest that the insights gained from covert research far outweigh the ethical objections. Denzin (1982) argued that researchers have the right to observe anyone in any setting because the evidence gathered can make a positive contribution to society. In other words, deceit and deception can be an integral part of getting at the 'truth'.

Douglas (1985) actually argues that sociologists in their search for truth should not let moral judgements get in their way, especially when studying those in power who frequently use lies and secrecy to maintain that power. We can illustrate these moral dilemmas by examining actual research that uses covert observation.

The most obvious examples are studies of groups involved in criminal or at least highly deviant activity. When Humphreys (1970) was making his study of homosexual activity in public lavatories (known in homosexual slang as 'tea-rooms') in the USA, there was no way in which he could have simply stood around watching what was going on. Nor, however, did he want to be an active participant. He resolved the problem by adopting the recognized role of 'watch queen' – he convinced the men who frequented the lavatories that he got his sexual kicks from watching other people engage in sexual activities and he got the trust of the men by acting as a lookout, warning them when strangers, particularly police, were approaching. The ethics of Humphreys' research has been questioned, especially in terms of his deliberate misrepresentation of his identity and his observation and encouragement of what were defined as criminal activities. However, Humphreys argues that the results of his research outweighed such ethical considerations because his research had positive consequences for those being studied in that his research findings reduced public and police stereotypes about homosexuals.

Festinger *et al.* (1956) joined a religious sect whose leader had prophesied that the world would end that year. They masqueraded as followers for months and were present at a meeting at which a flying saucer was supposed to arrive to whisk them to safety. Of course, the flying saucer failed to materialize and nor did the world end. However, Festinger and his colleagues continued in the group but sowed seeds of doubt and discontent by suggesting to people that the leader of the sect was a fraud. There are two main issues here. First, deception – should Festinger *et al.* have lied to the group about their motives? Second, Festinger's actions after the 'world-ending' meeting interfered with the natural dynamics of the group in that they attempted to manipulate the behaviour of the group. It was at this moment that Festinger's observation study turned into a social experiment, i.e. new variables were introduced by Festinger into the situation.

Holdaway (1983) takes another view of the ethical arguments. He was able to use the fact that he was a police sergeant (and a sociology graduate) to conduct a covert study of the police at work, and discusses the ethics of such research. He states that 'the argument that all individuals have a right to privacy (that is to say, freedom from observation, investigation and subsequent publication based on the investigation) is strong but should be qualified when applied to the police'. His conclusion is that 'In part, therefore, my covert research is justified by my assessment of the power of the police within British society and the secretive character of the force. . . . It is important that they be researched.'

The phases of ethnographic research

The stages of ethnographic research are even less distinct from each other than those of the survey, but certain phases can be identified.

Choice of topic

As with all research, the first decision to be made is the choice of topic and group to be studied. This choice will always be made as a result of the wider interests and basic curiosity of the researcher, and there is the usual interplay here between theoretical assumptions, areas of research interest and research method chosen (see p. 27).

Deviant behaviour has always been a popular topic for ethnographic research. Given the essentially secret nature of much deviant behaviour, those involved are unlikely to be willing to be interviewed, or at least to give truthful answers, in a survey. Deviants and groups of people who feel under threat are unlikely to respond enthusiastically to a researcher with a questionnaire. Okely (1983), in her study of traveller-gypsies, quickly found that a questionnaire administered to a large number of gypsies was hopelessly inappropriate for this particular study and soon switched to more ethnographic methods.

Clearly, if one is interested in deviant groups, and is convinced that the way to understanding their behaviour is to see the world from their point of view, the best way to achieve this is by becoming deeply involved in their way of life. Examples of such research include Wolf's (1991) research into biker gangs, Adler's (1985) study of drug dealers and smugglers, Bourgois (1995) who spent three years studying crack dealing, and Hobbs who carried out covert observation on petty criminals and CID officers in the East End of London, *Doing The Business* (1988), and on professional criminals at work and at play, *Bad Business* (1995).

This still leaves the problem of which particular deviant group to join, and whether that group is typical of all such groups. In practice, ethnographers tend rather to play down the question of whether their particular group is typical of others, but the reader must recognize that the choice of group is a kind of sampling, and the question of representativeness must arise. Selection of a topic and group is also affected by the fact that some groups have the power to refuse access to researchers. It is no surprise, therefore, that we have no ethnographic studies of powerful decision-making groups, in business or in politics, and many studies of relatively powerless groups.

Reviewing the literature

This is as important in ethnographic research as it is in any other style of research (see p. 31).

Joining the group

Having chosen what group or institution is to be studied, the researcher has to decide what their 'cover story' is going to be. Are they going to tell the people that they are studying them, and be 'overt' about their role as researcher, or are they going to act a part, conduct 'covert' research and never let on what they are doing? This will to some extent be based on the ethical considerations discussed above.

Whether the researcher's role is going to be covert or overt, the next problem is to gain access to the group being studied. There have been as many ways of doing this as there have been ethnographic studies.

Sometimes access to a group comes via an intermediary or gate-keeper who is close to the group in question and who can reassure the group about the motives of the researcher. Liebow (1967), a white researcher, was able to access a group of black Americans through an intermediary called Tally Jackson, who was to give his name to the classic book that Liebow finally wrote, *Tally's Corner* (1967). Similarly, Bill Whyte's classic study *Street Corner Society* (1955) was very dependent upon 'Doc', his key informant, who introduced him to the other members of the group. Sharpe's (1998) study of prostitution needed police co-operation to get her access to prostitutes working in three streets in which the police tolerated the practice in order to control it.

Barker (1984) had the unusual experience of being approached and invited to do research into a very closed group, in this case, a religious sect in which she was already interested, the Unification Church, known popularly as the Moonies. Sometimes, official gate-keepers like church officials can be very difficult because they can seek to impose controls on the research. However, Barker made it very clear to the Moonie hierarchy that the research would be done on her sociological terms. Moreover, the Moonie invitation had the advantage of guaranteeing their co-operation and she was given access to people, Moonie centres (i.e. she stayed in these for periods of time), workshops, seminars and documents.

Fielding (2001) argues that access-givers are 'the unsung heroes of ethnography' because these sponsors are crucial sources about the group or organization which the researcher is studying. However, he notes that it is important to also understand that some, especially institutional gate-keepers, may have an agenda of their own, and they may wish to control how you observe and what you observe.

When a researcher is investigating an institution of some kind, it is usually necessary to get permission from the authorities for the work to be done. Thus Burgess (1983), in his study of a secondary school, had to obtain permission from the chief education officer and the headmaster before he entered the school. However, this leads to the possibility that those being researched see the researcher as somehow connected with authority and change their behaviour accordingly. Corrigan (1979) felt it was important, in his study of the boys in an urban secondary school, to create a role for himself which was not threatening to them. In the end, in order to ensure the trust of the boys, he adopted the role of 'cockney writer', a role which was genuine, and which showed the boys that Corrigan was interested in them for themselves. Parker told his delinquent boys that he was 'at the university' and was conducting research which was going to criticize the police and the courts.

Some researchers have been able to make use of their own skills to gain access to a group. Becker's expertise as a jazz pianist made possible his study of dance musicians (1963) whilst Polsky used his ability at the pool-table in his study of 'pool-room hustlers' (1967).

Abrams and McCulloch (1976) found that the role of 'sympathetic outsider' enabled them to study communes in a way that was involved, detached, and not regarded by commune members as unduly threatening.

First phase of research

Having gained access to the group or institution being studied, the researcher enters the first phase of the research proper. In this he or she follows very broad lines of action, trying to be as open-minded and receptive as possible, seeing all the patterns that begin to emerge. The researcher is little different from anyone else joining a new group and trying to be accepted by them. We are all able, at a common-sense level, to identify what is acceptable behaviour in any new group. What makes the researcher different is that the purpose of making these observations is not only to become a member of the group but also to write an account of its way of life. To do this, the researcher has to remain detached from the group at the same time as becoming a member of it. This is the key to successful ethnographic research. Researchers have to monitor not only the actions and behaviour of the group members, but also their own activities, and they must cultivate self-criticism and self-awareness. The trick is to see the social context as the regular participants do, while at the same time remaining a detached observer of events. It has been suggested that, if a researcher is not sometimes surprised at what they observe, then they are failing to be as open-minded as they should. Holden's (2002) ethnographic account of the Jehovah's Witnesses illustrates the above very well. He noted:

As I became a more familiar figure at the Kingdom Hall (the official name for the Witnesses' place of worship), I realized that I was both subjectively involved on the inside and dispassionately collecting data from the outside. . . . Like an actor I felt I was performing and, at the same time, I was aware that the activities in which I partook were being carefully constructed by those with whom I had little in common. Needless to say, my relationships with individuals in the congregation were different. To some, I was a polite but skeptical academic with nothing other than a quasi-professional interest in their way of life. To the elders, I was an enthusiastic young man of apparently agnostic disposition who needed help in collecting what was to them rather futile information. To others still, I was a friendly acquaintance (rather than a friend) who, unlike most other outsiders, had a comprehensive knowledge of their mission and with whom they could hold an intelligent conversation.

(p. 6)

All researchers agree that it is important to remain inconspicuous at this stage. As Polsky (1967) said: 'Initially, keep your eyes and your ears open, but keep your mouth shut.' Whyte (1955) agreed and noted: 'As I sat and listened, I learned the answers to questions I would not have had the sense to ask if I had been getting my information solely on an interviewing basis.'

The other most obvious difference between the researcher and the ordinary new member of a social group is that the former must keep detailed and accurate notes and records of everything observed and every impression gained. This can be done in a variety of ways, but researchers are unanimous that it is essential to write up the events of a day before going to bed at night, or, at the very latest, the following morning. This entails taking notes wherever possible, without being too obvious about it. Fielding (2001) suggests an effective ploy is to develop the reputation of having a weak bladder which allow frequent visits to the toilet without arousing too much suspicion. Ditton (1977) used the lavatory as a place to make notes secretly and took his first notes on lavatory paper.

Clearly, to take notes openly and constantly is bound to affect the behaviour of a group. But is it really possible for researchers to remember details of conversations as they claim to do? Or all the details of complex and perhaps fast-moving events? Many researchers are surprised and delighted at their ability to remember conversations almost word for word. Pryce (1979) had to rely heavily on memory:

My method was to write down these observations as soon as possible after hearing or observing them. The rule of thumb I constantly exercised was to record them while they were still fresh in my mind, generally the same day. It was my practice never to record anything, especially conversations, after three days . . . it is surprising how efficient one's memory can become with practice.

(p. 299)

Fielding (2001) suggests that most people lose good recall of quite simple events after 24 hours and if conversations are to be recalled in detail so that they include quotations, they must be written down within hours. Covert researchers face these problems more acutely because they cannot be seen to be writing. Holdaway (1983) kept shorthand notes on a scrap of paper in the back pocket of his trousers. He also noted that he was very sensitive to discovery when writing up notes at the station. Parker (1974) found that in order to maintain the rapport he had with his delinquent boys he had to spend his leisure time drinking with them. The ensuing drunkenness made it difficult to record events although he insists that recording still took place despite his condition!

In any case, it must be recognized that these notes, however full and detailed, are only a selection from all the events that the researcher witnessed, and that this selection is made on the basis of what the researcher considers to be significant. This in turn means that there is sampling involved, and it is sampling based on the judgement of the researcher. As with the survey, the researcher's judgement about what is important must affect the outcome of the research.

Middle phase of research

As the research progresses, so ideas start to crystallize. Barker (1984) calls this the 'interactive' stage. The researcher begins to build relationships with people, and certain individuals emerge as 'key informants' for the research. The 'key informant' will often be the same individual who made possible the researcher's access to the group. These individuals can be quite influential and sometimes become almost a partner in the research. The most famous of these figures, 'Doc' in *Street*

Corner Society (Whyte 1955), literally became an assistant to Bill Whyte, and indeed gave Whyte another ethical problem, as both he and Doc came to see that Doc's behaviour had changed as a result of Whyte's work. Doc said: 'You've slowed me down plenty since you've been here. Now, when I do something, I have to think what Bill Whyte would want to know about it and how can I explain it. Before I used to do things by instinct' (Whyte 1955).

In this stage, the researcher will begin to penetrate the 'fronts' that are always put up for an outsider. The observer needs to cultivate a role that will establish trust and rapport with the group being observed so that what is observed is authentic. As Brewer notes 'ethnographers earn people's trust by showing a willingness to learn their language and their ways, to eat like they eat, speak like they speak and do as they do' (2000: 85). Brewer notes that trust takes time, and consequently researchers may have to spend considerable periods of time in the field so that people get used to their presence.

Fielding recommends the role of 'acceptable incompetent', i.e. acting in a naïve fashion so that group members feel obliged to explain things to them. Marvasti (2004) suggests using interest in the respondents' culture and way of life to establish rapport because people are often flattered by the attention. Marvasti also suggests self-disclosure is another way in which rapport can be maintained. 'Telling people about yourself is a very natural way of starting friendships and gaining trust, but don't overdo it. Talking too much about oneself can get in the way' (p. 49). Some researchers believe that self-disclosure is part of the ethical commitment that they have to their respondents. Moreover, being evasive and mysterious is going to undermine trust. However, as van Maanen (1982) warns, not every researcher can expect to be liked by all members of the group, and trust may be unachievable.

Fielding (2001) notes that these considerations underpin the choice between overt and covert forms of observation. He argues that there is probably no better way than covert observation to understand how members of the group give meaning to their experiences. The researcher can be fairly certain that what is observed is natural and not an artificial reaction to the presence of the researcher. However, playing a covert role is extremely demanding. The researcher may not be able to ask certain crucial questions without arousing suspicion. Moreover, what you can and cannot observe is restricted by the role. The researcher is unlikely to occupy a role that allows free movement. Wandering beyond the limits expected by the role may be dangerous. In this sense, then, as Gomm (2004) notes 'participating can get in the way of observing' (p. 229).

Overt observers, on the other hand, probably have more flexibility in where they can go. They can openly ask questions and write up notes. They usually have an informant to fall back on with whom they can discuss their observations. However, overt observers need to find a balance between merging into the background so that they do not disrupt the natural rhythm of the group and occupying an active role that does not cause behaviour around them to change. Julia O'Connell Davidson (O'Connell Davidson and Layder 1994), for example, in her study of prostitution took on the role of receptionist to a group of prostitutes. The prostitutes knew she was a researcher although their clients did not. Gomm (2004) also notes that overt researchers often get too close to their informants and consequently there is a danger that the observer only sees the world through the eyes of some of the group or that the observations are coloured by their prejudices.

Covert research is seen by some critics to increase the possibility of the researcher's 'going native'. This expression originated with the anthropologists, and refers to the possibility that the researcher will become over-involved with the people being studied, and so lose the detachment that is an essential part of the participant observer's role. Empathy therefore gives way to sympathetic bias which undermines objectivity. It is argued that overt forms of participant observation are less likely to experience this problem because the researcher occupies a visible professional role. Abrams and McCulloch (1976) in their study of communes, drew a firm line: 'our idea of participant observation extended to making beds but not to making love'. Fielding (2001), however, points out that another common problem of overt observation is 'not getting close enough' and consequently producing superficial data.

Another ethical problem which seems to characterize covert studies is involvement in crime. Fielding notes that 'observers often feel bound to help members in exchange for their tolerating the research' (2001: 151). This is a risk that is always present for covert researchers, such as Patrick (1973). Patrick, in fact, left his group abruptly when the violence became too much for him. Parker (1974) in his study of 'street kids' in Liverpool, *View from the Boys*, tried to demonstrate his loyalty to them and passed various 'tests' including acting as a look-out whilst they broke into cars, receiving stolen goods and so on in order to get their trust.

Polsky has been particularly critical of covert researchers in the field of crime who have attempted to act as one of the group studied. He argues (1967) that it is not a good idea to pretend to be a criminal because at some stage the criminal group will want to test the researcher's claim, and the consequences of this may be dangerous. Ken Pryce, the author of the acclaimed observation study of West Indian life in Bristol, *Endless Pressure* (1979), was murdered when he attempted to covertly investigate organized crime. Polsky argues that this danger is the main reason why such research should not be covert. If the people know from the start where the researcher draws the line, then the problem does not arise.

The choice whether to use covert observation is restricted by the social characteristics of the researcher. The social class, gender, age and ethnicity of the researcher may make it impossible to infiltrate particular situations, e.g. males are excluded from exclusively female situations or groups and vice versa. Sometimes, however, distinctive social characteristis are required to gain access to particular groups. Pryce, an African-Caribbean researcher, was able to access areas of St Pauls in

Bristol from which a white ethnographer would have been excluded. Studies of pupils in schools have benefited from the fact that researchers such as Corrigan and Willis were not substantially older than the people whom they were observing. Parker (1974) notes that his ability to blend in with the delinquents he was observing benefited from being in his early twenties, his untidy and informal dress sense, his ability at swearing, being able to understand 'scouse' dialect and being reasonably good at football!

Feminist researchers have identified a number of ways in which identity can affect relations between the researcher and researched in the field. On the positive side, females may be seen as less threatening than males, and consequently the observed group may behave more naturally in front of them. On the negative side, female observers may be treated in a patronizing way by male members of groups and receive unwanted sexual attention. Sharpe's (1998) observation of the policing of prostitution concludes that the research was completed *in spite* of police behaviour towards her.

Barker (1984) notes that the overt observer can follow up observations with informal interviews with members of the group. These are sometimes called 'guided conversations' and the role of the researcher is to ensure that the topics that have emerged as important during the observation are discussed. Generally these ethnographic interviews are flexible and reflexive in that such interviewers are active listeners who can develop questions as the conversation proceeds. The success of such interviews also depends on the rapport which has been built up over the course of the observation. Such interviews are sometimes useful as a tool of validation in that the observer can ask members of the group how they saw certain events to ensure that the researcher's field notes contain an authentic picture of what went on.

Final phase of research and writing up

In the last phase of the research, the researcher will be in a position to begin to test ideas about what is going on and to identify patterns of behaviour. It is now that the final form of the report or book begins to emerge, and the researcher has to begin to withdraw from the research group.

This stage includes the writing up of the research report. The people who have been studied will probably be interested in what is said about them, and this may affect what the researcher writes. Whatever promises of anonymity are given, the people involved will recognize themselves in the characters portrayed, and this may cause difficulties. If criminal activities are clearly involved, then the researcher has an ethical problem. Parker faced this dilemma in his study of a group of adolescent boys on Merseyside:

> The major problem in writing up is an ethical one, however. The fieldwork data basically fell into three categories: that which I felt could definitely be published, that which could definitely not be published, and that which I was unsure about. The third category was eventually broken up and distributed into the yes/no compartments through consultation with those involved and colleagues. Becker has pointed out in reviewing studies of this nature that publication will almost inevitably 'make somebody angry'. This is probably true; my main concern is that no harm comes to The Boys.
>
> (Parker 1974)

Coffield *et al.* (1986), gave all the young people in their study pseudonyms of their own choosing, but nevertheless decided to leave out a large amount of their richest data in order to further protect the identity of their sources.

As we have already seen, researchers who work within a scientific focus are sceptical about the objectivity of ethnographic research methods. In particular, they suggest that objectivity is undermined by the sheer volume of observational data which means that ethnographers have to make decisions as to what deserves their attention in terms of analysis and writing up. It is argued that selection of data is often based on conscious and unconscious ideological biases, i.e. data that supports the research hypothesis is given precedence over data that challenges it. For example, critics of Willis's (1977) study into the deviant subculture that develops among 'failing' boys in a secondary modern school, claim that he over-emphasizes their deviant behaviour at the expense of their conformist behaviour. Moreover, because much observational research is carried out by lone researchers, it is impossible to verify the data collected.

Some sociologists have attempted to counter this type of criticism by keeping research diaries which document the trials and tribulations of every stage of the field research. Brewer notes that nowadays 'reflexivity and the writing-up process are inseparable' (2000: 126). Reflexivity is a form of self-evaluation which involves researchers reflecting critically on how they organized the research process. As Dyson (1995) notes, it involves the researcher thinking about how a range of influences might have impacted on the writing up of the data and the validity of the findings. Such influences might include the power relations between the observer and observed, the social context of the research, mistakes made and even the impact of the researcher's own biography on the nature of the research findings. For example, Winlow (2000) talks about how his intimacy with North Eastern England working-class subculture and his working-class accent helped him to conduct his research into violent men.

Much of what Brewer calls the 'reflexive turn' has been inspired by the postmodern perspective which argues that ethnography should not be concerned with the pursuit of some universal truth because at best, accounts of social reality can only be relative, partial, partisan and selective truths. Specifically, ethnographic accounts are seen as autobio-graphical, i.e. they only tell us about the researcher's version of the observation, and they leave out other participants' experience of it. There is no doubt that such self-criticism is useful, especially for future researchers to learn from, but some sociologists have noted a worrying trend that the reflexive now seems to be taking precedence over the research process and findings. May (2001) argues that much reflexivity can read like 'introspective indulgence'.

Leaving the group

At some point, the researcher has to leave the group which they have been researching. An 'exit strategy' has to be devised and put into practice. This raises a range of ethical issues in relation to terminating friendships, leaving people without support on which they may have come to depend, and similar problems.

Brewer notes that exit strategies are now being given more attention by ethnographers because of codes of ethics. He argues that withdrawal from a group should be gradual and every effort should be made to avoid distress to informants. Some feminist researchers believe that contact should be maintained long after the research has finished. Paul Willis kept in touch with the 'lads' in his study *Learning to Labour* for many years afterwards. However, this is more difficult with covert research because the deception may cause deep hurt. It may also create the potential for reprisal. 'James Patrick' was sufficiently worried by the reaction of the Glasgow street gang to his work that his real name has never been revealed. When Roy Wallis left the Scientologists after carrying out covert research, he received threatening letters from members of the group.

Conclusion

Finally, this brings us to 'auto-ethnography' in which the researcher's personal experiences and feelings about the topic are used as data. As Marvasti (2004) notes, 'auto-ethnographers turn participant-observation inward, they observe and write about themselves as they participate in the real world' (p. 58). Auto-ethnographers are committed to emotional honesty, openness and, often, to changing society. A good example is Roseneil's (1995) *Disarming Patriarchy*, which is an account of the experiences of women who in the 1980s expressed their anti-nuclear weapon politics by camping outside the United States air-force base at Greenham Common in Berkshire. In addition to interviews with thirty-five women in order to elicit their memories of the camp, Roseneil accesses her own memories of Greenham and retrospectively observes her behaviour in the year she spent in the camp. As Devine and Heath (1999) note 'it is clear that the events she describes were all experienced at first hand: she was there, she was an active participant, and we see the camp through her eyes' (p. 184). Roseneil's auto-ethnography also involves taking a political stand – she rejects scientific objectivity and deliberately sides with the Greenham women. Auto-ethnography stresses reflexivity, too, and consequently Roseneil comments in a very honest account of how life at Greenham influenced both her sexual politics and her subsequent academic career.

The ethnographer's central concern is to provide a description that is faithful to the world-view of the participants in the social context being described. Explanations of social action may emerge from this description, but that is not the primary purpose. The test of its validity is whether the subjects of the research accept it as a true account of their way of life. The researcher must not impose any prior assumptions on the subject matter, and should allow any theory or hypothesis to emerge from what is observed and recorded.

It is in this that the great strength of ethnographic research lies. Behaviour is observed in its natural setting, and it is possible to make a study of social process, rather than being limited to the snapshot or series of snapshots of the survey researcher. The emphasis is on describing the meaning of the situation for those involved in it. What makes the work scientific is the care taken to avoid error, to be thorough and exhaustive, and to check and recheck all findings.

Further reading

The style of this research makes it very difficult for the student to get the feel of it through first-hand experience. On the other hand, much of it is very readable. The following studies are all recommended on the grounds that they are clearly written, interesting in their own right, and include discussions of the ethnographic research method:

Abrams and McCulloch (1976)
Adler (1985)
Barker (1984)
Becker et al. *(1961)*
Becker et al. *(1968)*
Benson (1981)
Bhatti (1999)
Bosk (1979)
Coffield et al. *(1986)*
Corrigan (1979)
Ditton (1977)
Foster (1990)
Hargreaves (1967)
Hobbs (1988) and (1995)
Holdaway (1983)
Holden (2002)
Humphreys (1970)
Liebow (1967)
McKeganey and Barnard (1996)
Okely (1983)
Parker (1974)
Patrick (1973)
Plant (1975)
Polsky (1967)
Pryce (1979)
Sharpe (2000)
Smith (1983)
Whyte (1955)

Williams (1989) and (1992)
Willis (1977)
Winlow (2000)

> *It is not necessary, though it is desirable, to read the whole book in order to understand the methods used. All these books include a discussion on the research methods used.*
>
> *If you have time to read only one book, make it Whyte (1955), or the new edition published in 1981. Failing that, Parker, Corrigan, Holdaway or Hobbs are recommended.*

Other ethnographic techniques

Ethnographic research is not only carried out by means of participant observation and unstructured interviewing. Other techniques are available for obtaining insights into people's world-view and social relationships, and some will be briefly described here.

Case-studies

As we have seen with observation, social research does not have to be based on a representative sample. A case-study can be carried out, using almost any method of research, though qualitative methods are the most popular.

A case-study involves the in-depth study of a single example of whatever it is that the sociologist wishes to investigate. This may be an individual, a group, an event or an institution. Such studies, normally involve the researcher using a range of research methods. Maguire and Bennett (1982) constructed a case-study of a convicted career criminal, 'Peter Hudson', using unstructured interviews, his autobiographical writings and court records, to gain an insight into the practice of professional burglary. Paul Willis (1977) constructed a case-study of a group of twelve working-class boys in a secondary modern school in the Midlands in his book *Learning to Labour* in order to gain an insight into why such boys 'fail' at school. He used a combination of participant observation and interviews with the boys, careers staff and employers. *Strike at Pilkingtons* by Lane and Roberts (1971) is an account of an event, an industrial dispute at one large firm in Britain, and tells the story of what happened, examining the strike from the points of view of management, shop stewards and strikers, using interviews, observation, documents and press reports. Brewer's (1991) study *Inside the RUC: Routine Policing in a Divided Society* is a case-study of an institution or organization, in this case a police force using interviews with senior officers as well as rank-and-file officers, oral histories from retired officers and official documents.

Case-studies make no claim to representativeness because the essence of the technique is that each subject studied is treated as a unit on its own. So, using the examples above, Maguire and Bennett did not claim that 'Peter Hudson' was a 'typical' burglar nor did Paul Willis claim, contrary to popular opinion, that all working-class boys behaved as his sample did. Lane and Roberts do not claim that the Pilkington strike was typical of other strikes. However, what all these sociologists maintain is that a vividly told story can make an important contribution to our knowledge and understanding of aspects of social life such as crime, educational under-achievement, strikes and policing. Such case-studies may prompt further, more wide-ranging research, providing ideas to be followed up later, or it may be that some broad generalization is brought to life by a case-study.

In a sense, any ethnographic study is a case-study, since all such research concentrates on a relatively small group or a single institution. However, many ethnographic studies claim that the behaviour of their research populations are typical of similar groups, while case-studies tend to avoid making this claim. Rather, the case-study occupies an area somewhere on the borders between social research and journalism.

The life-history

A 'life-history' or 'life-story' is a type of case-study in which the intention is to interpret a person's life using a variety of ethnographical techniques. The sociologist aims to construct the personal narrative of an individual who may be selected because he or she is remarkable in his or her own right (e.g. as an influence, in some way, on some aspect of social life) or because he or she is seen as a typical representative of a marginalized or 'invisible' social group. Feminist researchers such as DeVault (1990) have been keen on the life-history because feminist interviewing is concerned with producing narratives that capture women's lives in areas such as crime and deviance which have previously been ignored by a male-dominated sociology. For example, Carlen (1985) in her book *Criminal Women* focuses on the criminal experience of four women and their contact with the criminal justice system. Campbell's (1984) *The Girls in the Gang* highlights the experience of particular females who belonged to New York street gangs in the 1980s.

Much of the data that constitutes a life-history is based on the respondent's own words in that autobiographical details of the person are usually obtained through a series of unstructured interviews or conversations. This data is normally supplemented by examining personal documents such as letters and diaries, and by conducting further interviews with friends, colleagues and even enemies. The Chicago School, whose work was described on p. 91, were the first modern sociologists to use this technique which can be seen particularly in Thomas and Znaniecki's *The Polish Peasant* (1919; see p. 150). A recent example of this method is Brewer (1984) who conducted a series of interviews, involving several meetings, with fifteen former members of the British Union of Fascists which was an extreme right-wing political party in the 1930s.

The life-history appeals particularly to sociologists who argue that we need to understand how people interpret social reality by using methods that allow researchers to see the world through their eyes. Life-histories, therefore, place great importance on the person's own interpretations and explanations of their behaviour and as such, provide ethnographers with very personal and richly descriptive narratives which give us great insight into everyday social life across time. Moreover, the life-history constructs the past (or at least, a version of it) in order to cast light on motives for present-day behaviour and attitudes such as criminality. Miller (2000) has gone further and used life-histories to collect family tree data that tracks social change across time, place and generations.

The life-history is a useful tool of social research (especially when it is used in conjunction with other methods). An individualized focus can highlight critical events that might account for the direction which people's lives take, especially in regard to criminal activities. For example, by examining the life-histories of juvenile delinquents and comparing them with sociological theories and policy responses, we can evaluate the success or failure of our institutional responses to this social problem and adjust them accordingly. Furthermore the life-history can tell us something very vivid about the life of a type of person whom we may never meet, such as the commune members studied by Abrams and McCulloch (1976). We can see him or her as a person rather than as a stereotype. Moreover, the life-history may also be used as an initial guide for 'opening up' almost any area of research. Oscar Lewis's studies of poverty (1964, 1968) are an excellent example of this method, in combination with others.

A variation on the life-history is the 'oral history' which focuses exclusively on reconstructing the past. Oral history enables us to take account of those many aspects of history that are not recorded in documents. It puts a whole new perspective on the study of the past, placing the lives of ordinary and unknown people at the centre, rather than the activities of monarchs and politicians. Brewer (1990) calls this 'a view from below' (p. 14). This emphasis has made it particularly popular with feminist researchers.

Oral history does not have to be collected from the very old, though books like Ronald Blythe's *Akenfield* and *The View in Winter* are marvellous examples of such work, while Roberts (1984) covers a longer time-span. Oral histories can also be useful for revealing discrepancies between the official histories of institutions such as the police and the day-to-day experiences of serving in the force as recounted by retired officers. For example, Brewer (1991) used retired officer's oral recollections to construct a history of the Royal Ulster Constabulary which differed considerably from the official version in regard to the policing of the sectarian divide in Northern Ireland.

The problems of life-histories and oral history are fairly self-evident: they cannot be shown to be representative or valid. Plummer (1988) notes that the past can only be recalled through the perspective of the present and this raises questions of the accuracy of the recall of facts, and about the interpretive framework through which memories are recalled. This is subject to a range of possible biases and distortions including memory loss, economy with the truth, self-justification or glorification and the fact that 'big' life events may overshadow and render less important in the memory the rather more mundane and everyday events in which the sociologist may be more interested. People also have the unreliable habit of idealizing the past. However, Brewer (1990) argues that such problems can be overcome by adopting a critical attitude towards the data, by constantly looking for internal consistency, weighing up the relative merits of pieces of evidence and cross-checking details by using supplementary methods.

Time budgeting

In this case, the researcher asks the subjects of the research to keep a detailed diary over a given period. The subjects assist the researcher by observing and recording their own activities in regard to the timing, sequence, duration and location of activities and the people with whom the activities were performed. Such diaries can have an interpretivist aspect in that respondents can record how they feel about these activities.

The primary advantage of time budgets is their sheer comprehensiveness. Questionnaires are limited in comparison because in practice one can only ask about a limited number of activities which must be precisely specified in advance. Time budgets are able to capture the relatively informal activities that make up a person's day such as 'napping' and casual encounters, the minutiae of a person's day that cannot easily be uncovered by interview or questionnaire.

Community studies

As we have seen, ethnographic studies aim to describe the way of life of a society or group of people. Where that group is quite small, such as a street gang, the main method of data collection used will be participant observation, perhaps supported by a limited amount of unstructured interviewing.

If, however, the group to be studied is larger, then a wider range of methods will be necessary, and we are dealing with a 'community study'. The tradition of community research can be dated from the work of the Chicago School, which includes the classic studies of Muncie, Indiana, USA, carried out by the Lynds and published as *Middletown* (1929) and *Middletown in Transition* (1937).

Such studies involve a researcher or a team of researchers in studying a whole community of people, usually in a small town or village, or possibly part of a larger town. The method is always for the researcher to go to live in the community being studied, and to become involved with the residents as a participant observer, but the community researcher will also use a wide variety of other sources of data such as community-wide surveys, formal and informal interviewing and examining public documents.

The problems of this kind of research are those of all ethnography, but with some special features. The first is gaining access to the community in question. This may be done simply by taking up residence in the area, without saying anything to anyone other than the organization sponsoring the research. This was done by Gans (1967) in his study of suburban America. In contrast, Stacey's study of Banbury began with a public meeting in which the aims of the study were explained to the residents.

Then there is the question of how many researchers should be used. If there is only one, he or she will never be able to cover all aspects of community life, and may even be disqualified, by reason of age, sex, or colour, from participating in certain activities. Pryce (1979) in his study of St Pauls, a part of Bristol mainly occupied by African-Caribbeans, focused on males in this area because his social characteristics as an African-Caribbean male made it difficult to access groups of women for research purposes. For this reason, some community studies, such as the Banbury restudy (Stacey 1975) have used teams of researchers, taking care to include a variety of social types in their number. The more complex the society being studied, the more specialist groups it is going to have.

What role should the researchers take on? Should they become deeply involved in the community, and risk losing the detachment needed in such work? Or should they remain marginal figures, seen as threatening by nobody, but at the same time, therefore, not really getting to know anyone in depth? In a large community such a marginal role may be possible, and the researcher can move from one group to another without difficulty, but in a village, or in a small community in a larger town, it is essential that the researcher be 'placed' in some way. Frankenberg (1957), in his study of a small Welsh village, became the secretary of the local football team. Other writers have found that the role of 'author' is enough to see them through, especially in communities where such figures are familiar.

Lastly, the researcher has to consider the effects that publication of the book may have on the community portrayed in it, and particularly on any individuals who may feature. Of course, the author will usually give the community a fictitious name, and also change the names of all key informants, but those who know the community concerned, and certainly all those who live in it, will not have much difficulty in identifying who is who. In the case of a large community this may be less significant, but where a small community is described there can be no anonymity for anyone. Is the researcher's responsibility to the people he has studied, or to the people who will read the book? Is it a case of 'publish and be damned' or do certain ethical codes take precedence? Every community will have its secrets, and every individual in it will have views that they would not normally express to others, but do express to the researcher.

Community studies, like all social research, are limited in time. A community is always changing and evolving, and even a year's study (three years in the case of the Banbury study) barely touches on this process. Some studies have, therefore, been repeated some years later, in an attempt to see what changes have taken place. The Middletown studies mentioned above are examples of this. The Banbury study was also followed up fifteen years later (Stacey 1960 and 1975) and significant changes were found to have occurred.

The distinction between community studies and small-scale ethnographies is not always clear cut but generally speaking, the wider the variety of data-collection methods used, and the larger the group studied, the more we are dealing with a community study. Sometimes surveys overlap with community studies as in the case of Young and Willmott's (1957) *Family and Kinship in East London*, which is a survey of family life in this area but, at the same time, its specific locational focus gives it a community study feel. The point to recognize, of course, is that it is futile to waste time classifying studies into neat little boxes. As stated on p. 22, research studies in the real world often use a variety of methods, chosen for their suitability for the task in hand.

The best way to learn about community studies is to read them. We recommend Stacey's two books (1960 and 1975), and those by Gans (1962 and 1967). The latter have more humour.

Ethnomethodology

As was suggested on p. 4, ethnomethodology was originally presented, in the 1960s, as a radical alternative and challenge to conventional sociology. It is today less dismissive of other approaches to the study of social life and has found a niche as a specialized way of analysing how people make sense of, construct and confirm their world-view and their way of life. It is included at this point on the grounds that its central focus is on the meanings and understandings that people use to make sense of their everyday lives.

The central idea of ethnomethodology is that the orderliness of social life is not the result of people obeying social norms or giving way to social pressures, but rather that orderliness is attained by all those involved in working to achieve it. The orderliness is produced by the participants, on every occasion that they interact. For Garfinkel, the founder of ethnomethodology, social events are entirely the product of the actions of those 'members' involved at any particular moment. People perceive the world as though it were guiding and constraining them. Garfinkel's interest is not in whether they are right or wrong in perceiving it in this way, but rather in how they come to perceive it in this way, and what effect this perception has on their actions. People need to make enough sense of any social event to be able to act appropriately. Garfinkel's recommendation to sociologists is:

> Look around you and everywhere you will find ordinary persons going about their everyday business performing familiar, unremarkable activities. This mundane fact is the

very crux of the social world. The ability of members successfully to perform practical activities in collaboration with others is what makes the social world possible. Therefore, take these practical actions and examine them for how they are accomplished. You will find that the methods involved are complex and sophisticated, yet they are possessed (and require to be possessed) by pretty nearly everyone.

(in Cuff and Payne 1984)

Ethnomethodology has developed various ways of demonstrating these unwritten rules of social life, and of showing how they are continuously achieved by social actors. There is the disruptive experiment, invented by Garfinkel himself. In this, the ethnomethodologist deliberately disrupts the taken-for-granted routine of social life, and watches what happens. You will find an account of these 'experiments' on pp. 81–2.

It is in the area of conversational analysis, however, that ethnomethodology has made the greatest contribution. Given that social order is continuously worked at and achieved by members, the question arises, 'How is this done?' What is the main method that people use to achieve social order? The answer is 'conversation and talk', and this led ethnomethodologists like Harvey Sacks into detailed analysis of conversation as a practical accomplishment of ordinary people. His aim is to show what are the taken-for-granted rules of conversation and how we describe the world to one another so that we all make sense of it in similar ways. As a result, we are able to interact with each other. He is particularly interested in the way that words and sentences change their meaning according to the context in which they are said and heard, and in the ways in which we all fill in the unspoken background of what is said to us. To understand the meaning of what is said to us is a cultural accomplishment that we take for granted.

Ethnomethodologists do not take it for granted. They try to spell out how we do it. Schegloff has made studies of the rules of conversation in so far as they govern who speaks when, and how we know when it is our turn to speak. For example, what are the rules that govern the opening of a telephone conversation? And how do we end the conversation in such a way that both persons involved recognize that the end has been reached, and neither feels snubbed? Of course, sometimes we do feel that the other person has been rather abrupt in ending the conversation, and that is the moment when we should do our ethnomethodological analysis to identify what it was that they, or we, failed to do as part of bringing the conversation to a proper and recognizable end. If we can identify it, then we have identified a taken-for-granted rule of everyday life.

Ethnomethodologists have also made studies of what they call 'practical reasoning'. How do people arrive at conclusions about what is going on in a particular instance? This process occurs not only in everyday life, but has also to be carried out by scientists in the laboratory, or by coroners in coroners' courts (Atkinson 1978).

The developments in techniques for both sound and video recording have opened up another world of data to ethnomethodologists (and, for that matter, to all sociologists). Making a recording of, for example, people walking along the street enables the researcher to study the unwritten rules which apply when people are trying to pass each other on a narrow pavement. Atkinson (1984) made detailed analyses of politicians' speeches recorded on video. He identified the methods they used, of both speech and body language, to elicit applause from their audiences.

Newcomers to sociology may find it difficult to make much sense of ethnomethodology. Many old hands find it an extraordinarily obscure, though fascinating, activity. For the purposes of this book, the important point to grasp is that it is a way of studying social life that concentrates on the unwritten rules that make ordinary everyday social activity orderly, and tries to spell out these rules.

5

Secondary data

The data that is used by sociologists may be 'primary' or 'secondary'. Primary data is collected first hand by the sociological researcher, mainly through the use of research methods such as surveys, interviews, or participant observation. Secondary data is evidence used by sociologists as part of their research which has been produced for non-sociological reasons, either by organizations such as the state or by individuals. This type of secondary data usually takes the form of official statistics and various types of 'documents'.

Data from earlier sociological research

Sometimes, a researcher will use data from previous sociological studies as the basis for new work. The 1980 Black Report (Townsend and Davidson 1982) documented the pattern of health inequalities in Britain, drawing on sociological evidence collected in the early 1970s. The report prompted a mass of sociological research throughout the 1980s which was gathered together in 1987 in the form of a Health Education Council report, *The Health Divide* (Whitehead 1988), which documented growing inequalities in both mortality and morbidity rates across social classes in the UK.

Sally Power *et al.*'s *Education and the Middle Class* (2003) deliberately sets out to mirror Jackson and Marsden's 1962 research *Education and the Working Class*. Much of the empirical research carried out by Power *et al.* into the social backgrounds and educational aspirations of middle-class families and their children is based on previous research carried out by educational sociologists such as Bernstein, Halsey, Ball and others in the last forty years.

A great deal of past sociological research and the research tools used, e.g. questionnaires, interview schedules, etc. are now available to contemporary sociologists on data archives accessible via the internet. It is therefore now possible for contemporary sociologists to tap into extensive amounts of previously collected data based on large representative samples. This is obviously advantageous to researchers with very limited funds although it is important that such data is treated cautiously because there may be important discrepancies between past and present day researchers on how they define the concepts used in their hypotheses, how they select their samples, etc.

There are three on-line data archives sites which sociologists can access; the Data Archive (www.data-archive.ac.uk) holds over 400 sets of data. CASS or the Centre for Applied Social Surveys (www.natcen.ac.uk/cass) provides access to questionnaires from major surveys whilst Qualidata is the Economic and Social Research Council's Qualitative Data Archival Resources Centre and can be found at www.essex.ac.uk/qualidata.

Statistics

Official statistics

The concept of 'official statistics' refers to those statistics collected by the state and its agencies. These are assembled in various ways by a range of government departments and cover the whole spectrum of contemporary life including the economy, employment, crime, education, family and households, health, etc. Most of these official statistics are collated and published by the Office for National Statistics (ONS) which was formed when the Central Statistical Office was merged with the Office for Population, Censuses and Surveys in 1996. Data produced by the ONS is available on its website (www.statistics.gov.uk) as well as being published in statistical compendiums available in book and CD-Rom form such as Social Trends and the Annual Abstract of Statistics.

In any large, complex and centralized state, these figures are needed for planning and evaluating social policy. For example, knowing how many people aged between fifty and sixty are alive today, together with knowledge about the death-rate of this age group and their state of health, enables the state to plan future health care provision for the elderly. This does not automatically mean that the provision will be made, but it does make it possible to plan in the light of solid knowledge rather than guesswork. Any state that has a system of publicly funded welfare – and all modern industrial societies do – needs information about the population with which it is dealing.

There are several sociologically relevant sources of official statistics.

Registration In the United Kingdom, since 1837 certain life events have to be registered by law. The most obvious examples are births, marriages and deaths. These figures are collected continuously, and at any particular moment details of what is happening in terms of trends in the population or specific details such as a rise or decline in particular types of death, such as suicide, can be worked out.

The Census In the United Kingdom, a survey of the whole population known as the Census has been carried out every ten years since 1801 (with the exception of 1941). It was last carried out in 2001. It involves the distribution of a questionnaire to every household in the country. The head of each household, which includes people who are in charge of residential homes, hotels, etc., is required by law to fill in the questionnaire on behalf of everybody in the household, or at least to ensure that they fill in one for themselves. The questionnaire varies from one Census to another, but always includes questions about age, sex, marital status and all members of the household. It also asks about their work, their educational qualifications, whether people have moved house in recent years and about living accommodation such as the number of bedrooms, bathrooms and toilets there are in a house. (The Census form can be downloaded from www. statistics.gov.uk/census2001.)

In 1991, questions about ethnic background were asked for the first time, although there were complaints that the categories made available did not include (a) the Irish who are thought to be largest and oldest ethnic minority group in the UK and (b) people of mixed-race extraction. These omissions were rectified in the 2001 Census which also included for the first time a question about people's religious affiliation in order to gauge the size of the UK's religious communities, especially the Muslim community (although strangely, this question was not asked in Scotland). The 2001 Census also reflected changing family lifestyles in that for the first time people were invited to classify themselves as a 'partner' as an alternative to husband or wife.

In recent years, there has been keen debate about the usefulness of Census data, and the reliability of the methodology that underpins it. On the plus side, it is argued that the Census produces a wide range of important social statistics which help policy-makers across government departments to create evidence-based policies and to monitor their performance. It is argued that the Census can lead to a more effective and fairer distribution of economic and social resources because it has the potential to identify more specific social groups, such as ethnic minority or religious groups, and their needs and problems.

On the other hand, there are signs that the management of the Census is a logistical nightmare for the ONS. The validity of the 2001 Census data has been questioned because a shortage of staff led to incomplete questionnaires being accepted. Furthermore, it has been argued that the representativeness of the Census is questionable because large sections of the population did not fill it in. It seems that the ONS lacked the resources to follow up or re-visit people who did not return the form.

This lack of quality control can be illustrated in regard to the 1991 Census in that it is now accepted that over one million people went 'missing' from this survey, i.e. a substantial minority of people somehow avoided filling in the questionnaire. This was partly caused by lack of trust amongst the general public as to the state's reasons for gathering such data. Some people may be anxious to avoid official registration because they are involved in illegal activities or because they wish to avoid paying local or national taxes, despite the fact that contrary to common belief, the Census asks nothing about wealth or income. Others may object to what they see as an infringement of their privacy and civil liberties. All of these fears, despite the ONS focus on confidentiality, may be enough to undermine the representativeness of the survey population. For example, Westminster Council calculated in 2004 that the 2001 Census has under-estimated its population by 100,000 people.

Further reading

If you live in England or Wales, you can obtain the Census results for your locality by logging on to www.neighbourhood.statistics. gov.uk or e-mailing census.customerservices@ons.gov.uk or by ringing Census Customer Services on 01329 813800.

Other state surveys   The state conducts several other surveys at regular intervals, all of them on a sample basis. The General Household Survey is conducted annually, and the Family Expenditure Survey and New Earnings Survey are commissioned by government departments and carried out by the Office of National Statistics.

Government departments   Most government departments produce a range of statistics which paint a dynamic picture of UK society in terms of trends and patterns in behaviour relating to social class, age, gender, ethnicity, religion, etc. and how these social characteristics interact with each other. For example, the Department for Education and Skills annually produces statistics relating to performance in standard assessment tests, GCSE, A-level and university degrees which allow sociologists to examine levels of achievement across different social groups, e.g. boys and girls, regions and schools. Information published in regard to truancy, exclusion and setting can also assist sociological understanding of educational inequalities.

Other sources of statistics

Agencies other than the state produce statistics that may be useful for sociological research. Most large pressure groups run or commission surveys on their own special interests. Trade unions will usually have statistical data about the industries in which their members are working. Any commercial organization that is quoted on the Stock Exchange is supposed to publish a statement of its financial affairs annually, and these can provide a wealth of information for sociologists who are interested in economic affairs.

How can sociologists use official statistics?

Many sociologists take these statistics at their face value, and use them as a ready-made source of data for their research. They are cheap, readily available, cover a long time-span and are comprehensive in their coverage of social life. They may be the only source of data on the topic in question. It may also be possible to do 'before-and-after' studies. For example, official statistics can be compared and contrasted before and after a specific piece of legislation, e.g. the Divorce Reform Act of 1971, to ascertain the 'effects' of such a change on marital breakdown. Official statistics on education and health, in particular, have formed the basis of much comparative analysis.

Many sociologists in the past have been attracted by the positivist characteristics of official statistics. It is assumed that they have been collected in a scientifically reliable and objective fashion, and consequently that they deal in 'facts'. For example, official criminal statistics in both the UK and USA indicate that crime is a male and working-class phenomenon. An uncritical acceptance of these criminal statistics led to the emergence of several theories of criminality in the 1950s and 1960s which viewed working-class culture as pathological, i.e. as naturally inclined towards criminal practices.

However, there may be problems. Since the statistics are collected for administrative purposes, the definitions used and the classifications made are often unsuitable for sociological research. It is not easy to make all the correlations that are needed. It is often not possible to check the accuracy of the figures. For example, it is assumed that registration of births, marriages, divorces and deaths is the most accurate of official data. However, while it is probable that the number of births recorded is as accurate as we are likely to need, the increasing numbers of people electing to live together rather than marry and the cultural and religious resistance to divorce in some quarters of our multicultural society undermines the validity of the picture of social life that the statistics purport to give us. Moreover, even death statistics do not escape this criticism.

Sociologists such as Atkinson (1978) and Taylor (1982) have illustrated that official suicide statistics probably underestimate the real UK suicide rate because coroners are afforded too much freedom in their investigations of suspicious deaths and because the existence of the 'open' verdict means that coroners will, sometimes in the face of fairly strong evidence, avoid a suicide verdict in order to lessen distress to the family of the deceased.

The work of Atkinson, in particular, has drawn sociological attention to the view that most official statistics are social constructions. What this means is that they are not simply facts or records of real phenomena. Rather official statistics are the end process of a series of relationships between social actors who are engaged in a constant process of interpretation and negotiation. This interpretivist critique of official statistics points out that a suicide (and therefore a suicide statistic) is merely a label imposed on a particular type of death by a powerful individual, i.e. a coroner (or a coroner's jury) after he or she has interpreted a range of clues as to the motives of the dead individual. The coroner's interpretation can be negotiated by a range of other social actors, for example, the pathologist who carries out the post-mortem, the police officer who investigates the scene of the death, the coroner's officer who investigates the biography of the deceased looking for profound events and experiences that could initiate suicidal action, the relatives who give evidence at the inquest as to the most recent state of mind of the deceased and even the deceased themselves, through the decision to write or not to write a suicide note. It is no wonder, then, that interpretivist sociologists suggest that the study of the social process of categorizing suspicious deaths as suicide is just as important as studying why people choose to kill themselves.

Similar observations can be made in regard to the official health statistics. Most health statistics, for example, are the result of people deciding that they are ill, and successfully convincing a doctor of this. If the doctor does not agree with them, then they do not go into the health statistics produced by the National Health Service. In other cases the doctor may, as a result of a routine check, say you are ill even though you do not feel it. It is not, therefore, the 'fact' of illness that produces the statistic – rather it is the interaction between individuals and the interpretation and negotiation that emerges from this interaction that results in someone being labelled 'ill' and becoming a statistic.

The example of crime statistics

In recent years, the official UK criminal statistics have come under sociological scrutiny by interpretivist sociologists who argue that the picture of crime and criminality that they paint is both unreliable and lacking in validity. It is argued that such statistics tell us very little about crime and criminals but that the study of the social construction of such statistics can tell us a great deal about the social actors involved in their collection especially victims and powerful interest groups such as politicians and civil servants, the police and the courts.

The interpretivist critique of the official crime statistics notes that a 'dark figure' of unrecorded crime exists. Clearly, many crimes go unrecorded, either because they are undiscovered, or because they are not reported to the police. Many crimes depend for their success on being undiscovered, such as fraud and embezzlement. However, others are not reported because of how the victim interprets the crime. For example, a victim may feel embarrassment or fear (rape, domestic violence, child abuse). They may feel that there is little the police can do about it (vandalism, shoplifting), or they may interpret the offence as not very serious anyway. Some crimes, of course, are interpreted as having no victim as such (drug abuse, soliciting, under-age sex).

Both property and violent crime increased dramatically between 1971 and 1993. However, interpretivist sociologists are sceptical that this figure indicated a real rise in crime. Instead they argue that the increase was due to a rise in the reporting of crime by the general public as they became more intolerant of certain types of crime because of changes in both the economy and social attitudes. For example, it is argued that increased affluence means that since the 1960s we have become a more materialist society. We are more likely today to own a car and a wide selection of consumer goods. Moreover, property has become more important to us and this is reflected in greater take-up of insurance. Consequently, we are more intolerant of theft of our property and therefore more likely to report it to the police. Indeed, insurance companies require that the police allocate a ' crime number' before they will meet a claim for theft, burglary or damage to property. Social attitudes towards violent crime may also have changed. For example, women in 2004 are less likely to put up with domestic violence, and despite the view that this is still the most under-reported form of violence in UK society, they are more likely to report it compared with the past, especially as the state and agencies such as the police offer more support and sympathy.

Various techniques have been developed to compensate for the problem of incomplete crime statistics. Sociologists working for the Home Office have been responsible for the British Crime Survey (BCS), a type of victim survey which has been used alongside the official criminal statistics to give a more complete picture of crime in the UK. The BCS was first conducted in 1983 and is now conducted annually. It involves sending a questionnaire to a nationally representative sample of over 10,000 households drawn from the Postcode Address File asking respondents to report all crimes committed against them, whether reported to the police or not in the past year. Other sociologists such as Newburn and Hagell (1995) and Campbell (1984) have used 'self-report' studies, i.e. anonymous and confidential questionnaire-based surveys which invite mainly young people to say what crimes they have themselves committed. Both types of survey show a far higher figure for crimes committed than do the official statistics produced by the police. For example, the BCS has consistently found that only one in four crimes is actually reported to the police whilst in 2001 it was estimated that only 54 per cent of reported crime was actually recorded by the police.

According to the interpretivist critique of the official criminal statistics, it is important to examine the administrative and cultural practices of the police. In fact, some sociologists go as far as suggesting that the official criminal statistics tell us more about the attitudes and behaviour of police officers than they do about criminality.

First, in regard to administrative practices, it is important to understand that what goes into the official statistics is often defined by civil servants and the priorities of politicians. For example, police officers are dependent upon the counting rules set out by civil servants at the Home Office. These rules define what counts as crime and over the last 20 years have changed frequently. In 1999, violent crime rose according to the statistics but this was largely due to a change in definition of what the Home Office defined as assault within the counting rules. Police officers may also exercise discretion in what they record as crime depending on how much national or local pressure they are under to clear up crime. Politicians, too, contribute to crime rates by changing laws or by instructing the police to stamp down hard on certain types of behaviour. It is likely that juvenile delinquency rates will rise sharply in the next few years as the police respond to political pressures to deal with anti-social behaviour in cities, especially that linked to drinking culture.

The activities of politicians and the police are also affected by public opinion, which is itself fed by the mass media response to the published statistics which are often characterized by 'moral panic', i.e. sensationalist and exaggerated headlines and stories which result in increased public anxiety about crime. This can increase people's willingness to report certain crimes, which has also contributed to recent increases in the official statistics for racial attacks, domestic violence and child abuse.

Second, it is argued that the official criminal statistics reflect police street or beat practices rather than criminal behaviour.

It is assumed that all members of society are policed equally in the eyes of the law, but the evidence suggests otherwise. In particular, a disproportionate number of working-class and African-Caribbean people are arrested, charged and convicted. For example, the official criminal statistics indicate that African-Caribbeans who only make up 2.3 per cent of the British population make up one-tenth of the male prison population.

A range of mainly observation-based sociological studies have suggested that negative stereotyping by officers on the streets may lead to powerless social groups such as young blacks and working-class whites being labelled as 'threatening', 'suspicious' and 'potentially criminal' and being subjected to greater police scrutiny than other social groups. The areas in which they live may also be subject to a greater level of policing. Such attention is likely to lead to a greater level of interaction between police and suspects, and possibly conflict, leading to arrest. In 2002, the statistics showed that young black people are eight times more likely to be stopped and searched by the police than young white people. Interpretivist sociologists have therefore concluded that the official criminal statistics tell us little about crime but a great deal about modern policing. In 1999, the Macpherson Report into the death of the black teenager, Stephen Lawrence, concluded that the London Metropolitan Police force was guilty of 'institutional racism' in their dealings with the black community. Sociologists such as Holdaway (2000) have suggested that the occupational culture of policing in the UK is predominantly masculine and white, and the official criminal statistics are the end product of the racial stereotyping of ethnic minorities that such a culture encourages.

The statistics may also reflect similar biases in the criminal justice system. For example, Hood (1992) studied 3,300 cases heard at the West Midlands Crown Courts in 1989 and found that young African-Caribbeans were more likely to be sent to prison than their white peers for the same offence. Some feminist criminologists have similarly observed that women who do not conform to a feminine stereotype are more likely to receive custodial sentences. Interpretivist sociologists therefore conclude the official criminal statistics may tell us more about judicial attitudes towards particular social groups than crime itself.

The social constructionist argument advanced by interpretivist sociologists illustrates the problematical rather than scientific nature of official criminal statistics. Figure 5.1 illustrates the process by which a criminal action may or may not be transformed into a criminal statistic. Croall (1998) notes that criminologists estimate that for every 100 crimes committed, only 27 are recorded by the police and only 5 are cleared up in the form of a caution or conviction.

A critical view

So far, we have seen the argument that is put forward by those who stress that official statistics are constructed rather than merely collected.

Sociologists influenced by a more Marxist approach accept the importance of this work, but maintain that it does not go far enough. For them, the important point is that these figures are produced by the state. The state is seen not as a neutral body, but as the key agency in the promotion of the interests and values of the ruling class in capitalist society. They wish to show how official statistics (state-istics) contribute to keeping the dominant class in power, by presenting information in ways which do not harm their interests.

They are not saying that the Office for National Statistics is engaged in some deep-laid plot against the working class. Rather, they argue that since the role of the state is to defend and justify the capitalist system, then official statistics must play their part in this.

At one level, this may simply be a matter of 'massaging' the statistics, something in which all governments engage. You do not have to be a Marxist to see that the official unemployment statistics include only those who are signing on at Job Centres

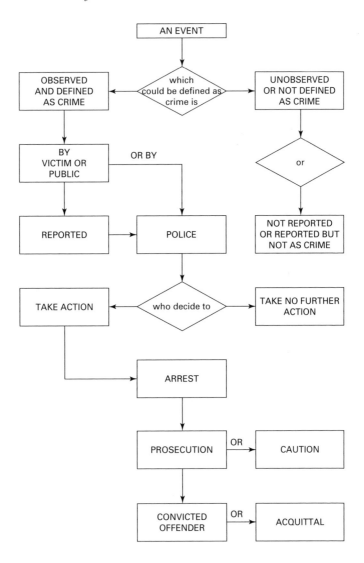

Figure 5.1 The social construction of criminal statistics
Source: Croall 1998: 16.

and are eligible for benefit. They therefore exclude married women, people who have retired early, those on training courses, those who have returned unwillingly to school or college because they cannot find jobs, those in temporary work, and others. Governments are constantly changing the criteria of what counts as 'unemployment'. In fact, since 1975, various British governments have changed the official definition of unemployment twenty-seven times.

A more subtle aspect of this argument concerns which statistics are collected and which are not. There is a great deal of information available about fire damage to property, but little on diseases related to industrial work. The figures on homelessness are vague and misleading, but those on new homes constructed are carefully recorded. We know more about social security 'scrounging' than we do about income tax evasion. We know more about the poor, who have to fill in forms of all kinds in order to receive benefits, than we do about the rich, who have to declare their tax position only to the taxman, in strict confidence.

Then there is the way in which the statistics are presented. The Registrar-General's scale of social class, used up to 2000 and the new register of social class introduced thereafter, the National Statistics Socio-Economic Class (NS–SEC), is based on people's employment. From a Marxist standpoint this ignores and therefore obscures the real basis of social class, which is the ownership of productive wealth.

Another line of argument emphasizes how women are rendered invisible in these statistics. In addition to being under-counted in the unemployment figures, until 2000 a woman's class was determined by that of her husband. It is still the case in 2004 that official definitions of employment and unemployment do not classify full-time housewives as 'at work'.

We can illustrate the political nature of official statistics by examining crime statistics again. Marxists argue that the capitalist state collects and constructs criminal statistics in order to serve the interests of the capitalist class that controls it. Box (1987) argued that the criminal statistics are used to criminalize the activities of powerless groups such as the working-class and ethnic minorities. This scapegoating distracts the general public from the real problems of capitalist societies such as inequalities in wealth and income as well as justifying the introduction of more social controls, e.g. more policing and laws. Moreover, the official criminal statistics construct in the public mind what is defined as criminal behaviour. Consequently, the activities of powerful interests, e.g. failure to maintain safe working conditions for employees or polluting the environment, which may result in death and injury are not defined as serious because they are not officially defined as criminal and do not appear in the statistics.

Using examples such as these, it is argued that the processes by which statistics are produced, or not produced, and the way they are presented, follow a pattern that is organized around the exploitation of one class and sex by another in capitalist society (Irvine *et al.* 1979)

Documents

McDonald (2001) defines documents as

> things that we can read and which relate to some aspect of the social world – official reports, for example – but there are also private and personal records such as letters, diaries and photographs, which may not have been meant for the public gaze at all.
>
> (p. 196)

As McDonald indicates, there are a number of different types of documents that can be accessed by sociologists. These include contemporary and historical official reports, e.g. the Macpherson Report (1999) into the death of Stephen Lawrence or the Hutton Report (2004) into the death of Dr David Kelly as well as reports commissioned by research organizations such as the Joseph Rowntree Foundation or charities such as Oxfam, Age Concern and Shelter. Documents can also be made up of the private and personal papers of specific individuals, for example, the diaries of the MPs Tony Benn and Alan Clark have given us sociological insight into the day-to-day political process. Mass media print products such as newspapers, magazines, adverts and comics as well as audio and visual products such as music, films, radio and television programmes and commercials, as well as pop videos, are all forms of documentary evidence which can be utilized by sociologists. According to McDonald, literature and art, too, can constitute social documents. Sociologists have therefore accessed novels, poetry, autobiographies, biographies, paintings and even gravestones for secondary data.

An interesting and unique example of a document is the suicide note. O'Donnell *et al.* (1993) accessed the suicide notes of people who had killed themselves on the London Underground in order to explore the range of social meanings that underpin the decision to kill oneself as well as the effect of such notes on the coroner's final verdict.

Scott (1990) notes that 'the invention of magnetic and electronic means of storing and displaying text should encourage us to regard "files" and "documents" contained in computers and word processors as true documents' (Scott 1990: 12–13). Consequently, sociologists need to think about how they can access the documentary evidence contained on the internet and world-wide web in a reliable and valid fashion.

McDonald argues that documents are 'socially produced' by organizations or individuals for reasons other than sociological research. This concept of 'social production' refers to the view that although documents are often presented as objective statements of social fact, they actually reflect the values and norms of the society or social group in which they are produced. Thus such secondary data can give sociologists tremendous insight into the organization of societies and cultures at particular points in time.

McDonald notes that whatever form documentary secondary data takes, research into it has all the deductive excitement of the detective story. However, it also requires a great deal of hard work because documents can be an untrustworthy source of evidence for the sociologist. Nothing can be taken for granted – the reliability, validity and representativeness of such evidence needs to be constantly checked.

Types of secondary document

The range of documentary secondary data available to the sociologist to use is vast. However, it can be grouped into six broad and sometimes overlapping categories:

- public or official records
- personal documents
- biography and autobiography
- literature
- historical documents
- print and visual media.

Public or official records

In modern societies written records are kept by all kinds of agencies and some may be available to social researchers. The state, in addition to producing official statistics, produces a wide range of documentary records. Laws, statutes, White Papers, Hansard (a verbatim record of what is said in debate in the Houses of Commons and Lords), public inquiry reports, ministerial records, political speeches, administrative and government committee records, at both national and local government level, and the content of various government department websites are all examples of the sorts of official documents available to the sociological researcher. School records, parish records, social work records, health records, police records, court records are also official documents, although in order to protect the privacy of those whose lives are recorded, the material may be kept confidential for some years, or may be available only in a form where individuals cannot be identified. For example, some documents may be protected by the Official Secrets Act and therefore be closed or only be partially available for research use.

There are also official histories that are commissioned by government, as well as the official reports of public inquiries. It is interesting to speculate on how future social researchers will use the Scarman Report into the civil unrest in British cities in 1981, or the Macpherson Report of 1999 which concluded that institutional racism existed at all levels in the London Metropolitan Police. The Black Report into inequalities in health (Townsend and Davidson 1982) has already passed into the main body of research, though it was commissioned and published, albeit unwillingly, by government.

Commercial firms, too, keep records of their decision-making procedures and financial transactions. Not all these are easily or indeed ever available to outsiders, but they should still be considered as potential sources of data, bearing in mind that they are produced as by-products of social, economic and political processes.

Personal documents

Ken Plummer (1983) notes that

> the world is crammed full of personal documents. People keep diaries, send letters, take photos, write memos, tell biographies, scrawl graffiti, publish their memoirs, write letters to the papers, leave suicide notes, inscribe memorials on tombstones, shoot films, paint pictures, make music and try and record their personal dreams. All of these expressions of personal life are hurled out into the world by the millions and can be of interest to anyone who cares to seek them out.
>
> (p. 13)

As we can see from Plummer, personal documents cover a great deal of ground. However, the main sociological focus has been on private papers, i.e. letters, diaries and autobiographies. These are first-person descriptions of social events or every-day life, written by an individual who was involved in or witnessed those happenings and can provide a very subjective and intimate picture of social behaviour and attitudes. Usually, personal documents are unsolicited, i.e. they are not produced with social research in mind.

Letters

The first major piece of sociological work that relied on letters was Thomas and Znaniecki's *The Polish Peasant in Europe and America* (1919). In this study of the migration of Polish peasants to the USA, Thomas and Znaniecki relied heavily on first-hand accounts supplied by people who had been directly involved. They placed an advert in a Chicago newspaper saying they would pay 10–20 cents for letters received from relatives. Thomas and Znaniecki used these letters, as well as life-histories obtained in interview and a specially com-missioned autobiography, in order to identify the themes that underpinned peasant life in early twentieth-century Eastern Europe and how Polish identity was revived by migration to the USA.

A recent piece of research that focused on letters was carried out by Valentine (1998). It examined the negative imagery of homophobic letters received by the researcher herself in order to make observations about sexual harassment and the nature of public and private space.

Hitchcock (1995) argues that it is important to understand that letters are designed for consumption by a third party. Consequently, the description of events by the letter writer may be geared to persuading someone else to accept an inter-pretation of reality that may be at odds with competing oral or written versions. Plummer notes that

> every letter speaks not just of the writer's world, but also of the writer's perceptions of the recipient. The kind of story

told shifts with the person who will read it – witness the different letters produced by Robert Burns to his mistress, his friends and his wife on the same day.

(1983: 23)

Moreover, those in receipt of letters may attempt to control or censor access or content in order to protect the reputation of the writer.

Hitchcock argues that sociologists have tended to approach letters with suspicion. However he notes that they can have sociological value if it is accepted that letters are texts to be interpreted rather than being taken at face value as a reflection of reality. It is therefore important to pay attention to the dates of letters and the sequence in which they are written, to investigate the social characteristics of both writer and recipient(s), to check whether the letter is typical of other letters of the time and the writer, to cross-reference to other data associated with the writer in order to check the authenticity of the letter, and finally, to be vigilant for hidden messages, etc.

Diaries

Diaries are generally unsolicited and some sociologists have used these to great effect. For example, Valerie Hey (1997) conducted a participant observation study of girls' friendships in two London schools. Her positive research relationships with the girls led to her gaining access to a unique form of personal document, i.e. the notes that the girls passed to each other during their classes. Some girls also offered her their diaries to read. Hey argues that these two forms of writings gave her real insight into the 'extensive emotional labour invested by girls in their friendships' (p. 50). Berman (1995) used the diary of a British cancer victim to explore attitudes towards death.

However, it is important to acknowledge two characteristics of diaries which distinguish them from other personal secondary documents. First, the diary can be a primary research tool.

Some diaries have been deliberately commissioned by sociologists in order to record particular events and/or to investigate how research subjects interpret social reality. In this sense, the diary can be seen as a type of self-administered questionnaire. Moreover, sociologists such as Dyson (1987) have championed the research diary as an important ethnographic resource in that it can give important insights into the research process (see p. 116).

Second, diaries are often produced by public figures, e.g. politicians for public consumption. Material written in the hope or the expectation that it will be published is going to be different from material that is never expected to be read by anyone other than the author and perhaps a close friend. Such 'public' diaries are in danger of being idealized and self-justificatory.

A variation on the diary in the USA is the high-school yearbook. Giordano (1995) analysed a sample of about 7,000 inscriptions made by students and concluded that these revealed a great deal about the rules underpinning adolescent friendship networks.

Biography and autobiography

The autobiography and biography can offer useful insights for the sociologist so long as they are approached with caution. It has to be remembered that the autobiography is a product of memory or as Harré notes, it 'must be constructed from a past which must be revived before it can be described' (1993: 220). The biographer, on the other hand, draws on whatever materials are available to present an account of a person's life and achievements. However, the final draft is the author's interpretation of documentary evidence (including the subject's own interpretation embodied in letters or diary entries) and the views of relatives, friends and colleagues who may have been interviewed. For example, Albert Goldman's *The Lives of John Lennon* (1988), which portrayed the ex-Beatle as a drug-addicted monster riddled with self-hatred, was criticized because of its selective use of sources, i.e. Goldman mainly talked to people who had come into some sort of conflict with Lennon and his wife. Both autobiography and biography, then, contain the potential for bias and distortion.

Gomm (2004) notes that often autobiographies are 'stories' that people tell about their experience aimed at convincing their audience that they are 'likeable', and 'trustworthy'. Oakley (1993) agrees. She argues that biographies and autobiographies are no different from any other kind of book. People's recollections are always partial and, to some extent, fictional because it is one writer's perspective on what actually happened written in the context of justifying their role and actions.

Despite these misgivings, Hobbs (2000) argues that autobiography and biography have contributed positively to our understanding of crime and deviance today. He notes that sociological studies of British professional and organized crime are rare and so, to some extent, we are dependent upon biographies, autobiographies and true crime books for an insight into the motives of professional criminals. Hobbs notes that autobiographies by the likes of John McVicar, Mad Frankie Fraser and Freddie Foreman convey the 'attractions of a life of crime, the dynamics of masculinity at its heart, the role of violence and the importance of reputation, even within instrumental networks of criminal entrepreneurs' (p. 167).

Other sociologists have pointed to the crucial role autobiographies can play in exploring the intimate and private, especially that associated with family life, which may not be easily accessible using questionnaires and interviews. White (1998), for example, used autobiographies to explore experiences of childhood in different time periods and social contexts whilst Van den Hoonaard (1997) used them to provide insight into the experience of widowhood. Roberts (1971) is a rather special example of a biography in that it combines personal reminiscence of family and community life with careful historical research into poverty in Edwardian Manchester.

Literature

Novels and plays can be useful sources of information for the sociologist, especially in terms of past cultural practices. For example, by reading the novels of Jane Austen, we can learn a great deal about patriarchal practices in eighteenth-century England and the very complex social rules that governed social relationships, especially between men and women. The socially observant drama of nineteenth-century writers such as Dickens and Hardy can shed light on urban poverty and rural life, respectively, in this period. The painstakingly detailed historical research carried out by contemporary writers such as that found in Peter Ackroyd's novels (as well as his factual books) on London or Patrick O'Brian's books on the Royal Navy at the time of the Napoleonic Wars provide sociologists with cheap, accessible and accurate detail about past periods which can be used in a comparative sense. However, some sociologists, notably Filmer (1998) argue that most classical literature reflects the values and interests of the cultured social elite for which it was produced and therefore can be unreliable as a sociological source. However, does Filmer's criticism hold true today when books such as the Harry Potter series sell millions of copies? Feminist sociologists such as Lobban (1974) and Best (1993) have felt that the content of children's books can further our sociological understanding of social processes such as gender role socialization. Novels can therefore be used as a topic for study in themselves, quite apart from their value as data to be used in studies of the social worlds which they describe.

Historical documents

Whether they are statistical or textual in nature, many secondary forms of evidence concern the past and are therefore historical documents. Past events in living memory can be researched using primary research methods such as questionnaires and interviews (although memories may be selective or shaky), but beyond this temporal point sociologists are dependent upon the sorts of documents listed above, especially personal documents, novels, autobiographies or public documents to give insight into British cultural life in the past.

Sociologists have particularly used historical documents in studies of family life. Peter Laslett (1977), using parish records between 1564 and 1821, questioned the view that extended families were common before the industrial revolution whilst Michael Anderson (1980) used early Census statistics from 1851 to show how extended family networks evolved from the need for mutual economic support in Preston.

Historical documents have also been used by sociologists in the study of crime and deviance. Studies of policing by Jones (1996) and Cockcroft (1999) have used a variety of historical sources to give insight into how modern policing methods have evolved. Jones's research focused on how fears, myths and prejudices about the police today in South Wales are rooted in nineteenth- and early twentieth-century police practices. Cockcroft compared historical texts with the accounts of retired police officers in order to see how 'official' and 'unofficial' accounts of policing differed. These differences between the 'factual' accounts of police histories and actual experience keenly illustrate the problem of accepting without question the view that documents reflect reality. Pearson (1983) explored a range of documentary sources going back to Victorian times to show that so-called 'golden ages' when crime was at a minimum were myths and that people's fears about crime in different historical periods were actually very similar.

Evaluating documents

Surprisingly, considering the wealth of documentary evidence available to sociologists, there are signs that documents have been neglected as a source of sociological data in recent years. Classical sociologists such as Marx, Weber and Durkheim were familiar with documentary research but as a major research tool in its own right, documentary research seemed to go out of fashion in the latter part of the twentieth century. Yet this type of research has many advantages for the modern-day sociologist, especially if combined in a triangulation approach with other more traditional methods of data collection. As Tim May (2001) notes, documents 'tell us about the aspirations and intentions of the periods to which they refer and describe places and social relationships at a time when we may not have been born, or were not simply present' (p. 176). In other words, documents allow us access to the past. Moreover, 'life-course documents' such as diaries, letters and biographies allow us access to intimate and private areas of social life which are difficult for sociologists to normally enter, for example, the areas of family life, or sexual practices, and attitudes towards 'taboo' subjects such as cancer, or death.

There has been a tendency from positivist survey-based sociology to dismiss documentary evidence as unscientific, unreliable and impressionistic. However, from an interpretivist perspective, documents can be seen as giving sociologists important insight into the social meanings that underpin social action and how people, particularly women and members of minority groups, interpret the social world in which they live. From this perspective, then, personal documents give sociological insight into subjective experience. They can tell sociologists a great deal about the way in which institutions and events are constructed and the interactions and interpretations that shape these. Furthermore, the results of documentary research can provide the basis for primary research.

Scott (1990) has provided sociologists with four criteria to be used when evaluating the usefulness of documentary forms of evidence.

Authenticity Scott argues that the first responsibility of the researcher using documents is to check the authorship. Papers may be deliberately falsified as in the case of the Hitler diaries which fooled the historian, Lord Dacre and the *Sunday Times* in the 1980s. McDonald (2001) notes that often problems of authenticity are not deliberate but instead the product of writers who 'may quite innocently or perhaps carelessly, convert fiction into fact or perpetuate the errors or deceptions of others'. On the other hand, Platt (1981), argues that the kind of documents in which sociologists are typically interested, are not known for problems of authenticity – there is little incentive to forge obscure parish records or a nineteenth-century report into factory conditions. However, she does argue that we should check whether authorship is genuine by asking whether the document makes sense or contains glaring errors, by asking whether different versions of the same document exist, whether there is consistency in literary style, handwriting or typeface, whether the document has been copied in any form, and whether the sociologist's version has come from a reliable source.

Credibility Scott argues that the sociologist needs to be certain that the document is free from error or distortion. In particular, the sociologist needs to examine when the account was written in relation to the events it describes. For example, was the author actually present at the event and writing immediately after it, when it was fresh in the memory, or was it written weeks, months or even years later, when the memory could have been distorted? Using this criteria, a diary entry may be more credible than an episode described in an autobiography. The motives of the source also need to be clearly identified, i.e. are they sincere or are they supporting a particular political position? McDonald notes that the social researcher should always ask 'who produced the document, why, when, for whom and in what context, so as to be assured of its quality' (2001: 205).

Representativeness Scott notes that the sociologist should ask whether the document is typical of a wider collection of potentially relevant documents that exist or may have existed. In other words, does the document give a complete or only a partial picture of the social phenomena in which the sociologist is interested? The sociologist needs to ask whether the document is whole or whether parts of it, or similar and related documents, have been deliberately or accidentally destroyed or been lost. This problem can be particularly true of personal documents – letters and diaries may be destroyed by the relatives of the famous and infamous in an attempt to 'save' reputations. Many sociologists studying suicide, believe that suicide rates underestimate the real level of these types of death because relatives often destroy suicide notes.

Written records of the past will, by definition, have been written by the literate, and they were often an unrepresentative minority of the population because only the reasonably educated kept diaries or wrote letters to each other.

Meaning　Scott notes that questions need to be asked about a document's clarity and comprehensibility because documents often have two layers of meaning, i.e. the surface or literal meaning and deeper, perhaps hidden, meaning. Scott suggests two questions should be asked: 'What is it, and what does it tell us?' In order to uncover all of the meanings contained in a document we need to look closely at the social context in which the document was produced.

Gomm (2004) argues that documents are an important sociological tool but notes that we must never forget that the writers of such documents are not writing with sociological research in mind. The purpose of their document is not only to present the 'facts' but also to celebrate their own achievement, to complain about the state of their world, to amuse and entertain, to defend themselves and even to mislead. It is therefore essential in analysing documents that the social context in which the document is produced is clearly understood by the sociological researcher. Gomm also notes that only some people write and publish, and consequently only some vantage points are represented in documents, i.e. these may not be representative of what really happened.

Furthermore, such writers will tell us what they think is important and interesting, and perhaps ignore what is of central interest to the sociological researcher.

Documents may be interesting for what they leave out, as well as for what they contain. May argues that documents should be viewed 'as media through which social power is expressed' (2001: 183), i.e. the powerful often use documents to persuade others to accept their legitimacy or to marginalize others. Therefore, what people decide to record also depends on the political context in which they exist, i.e. whether they have power or not, whether they are afraid of the consequences, etc.

Despite all these potential pitfalls, the use of documentary evidence, especially if combined with other methodologies, can prove illuminating in the sociological insights it can offer into the cultural practices and social meanings found in both the past and the present.

Print and visual media

During the last thirty years, there has been a steady growth of interest in mass media reports, both textual and visual, as a source of secondary data. This has obviously grown in tandem with the development of a sociology of mass media which has been concerned with the impact of mass media output on audiences. Early research, mainly by feminist researchers, into media representations of females in newspapers, magazines, comics and on television, especially advertising, has led to the emergence of an academic representations 'industry' which examines all sorts of media content for signs of patriarchy, racism, homophobia, ageism, disableism, etc.

In the field of crime and deviance in the 1960s, the pioneering work of Jock Young and Stan Cohen was important in establishing the existence of a relationship between crime reporting and the concept of 'moral panic', i.e. public anxiety about perceived threats to social order, and the effect of this on law enforcement, public attitudes and youth culture. Both

Cohen (1987) and Young (1971) used tabloid newspaper reports as their main documentary evidence, and this tradition has been continued by contemporary researchers such as Thornton (1995) and Redhead (1990).

Other sociologists such as David Buckingham (1996) and David Morrison (1999) have focused their attention on the potential effects that violence on television and in films may be having on impressionable young people whilst David Gauntlett (2002) has examined how young people may be using aspects of mass media to help construct their personal identities. All these media sociologists have used mass media reports in various visual forms as a means to get audiences discussing potential effects and uses.

Marxist researchers have despaired of the so-called dumbing-down of the television schedules as news and current affairs programmes and documentaries are abandoned in favour of *Big Brother*-type reality programming which does little to encourage people to think critically about the nature of our society. Research groups such the Glasgow University Media Group and Goldsmiths College constantly monitor media reporting of key political and social events, and argue that such reporting is often ideologically biased and partially responsible for shaping public opinion on issues as disparate as industrial action, the 'loony left', AIDS and how people feel about the under-developed world. For example, research by Philo (2000) examined television news reports about the developing world and concluded that this helped shape negative public perception in the UK about this part of the world because news stories were almost entirely negative.

Analysing and evaluating media reports

The main method used by sociologists for analysing media reports, whether they are textual or visual, has been 'content analysis' which started its methodological life as a research tool which counted the frequency of particular words, images or category of articles. This type of content analysis is still used but has been superseded by more qualitative versions which aim to focus on the textual and thematic analyses of media texts, i.e. the meanings, both literal and hidden, that lie behind the use of words or visual images.

Quantitative or formal content analysis

Formal content analysis is essentially a quantitative method. In its most simplistic form, the importance of a topic in a media report is measured by the number of times it is mentioned, the size of the headlines relating to the topic, the number of column inches dedicated to it and the size and nature of the photographs accompanying the article.

Most researchers will operationalize the topic they are examining by breaking it down into a number of codes or categories which are then entered onto a content frame or schedule that can be used to 'tick off' the category once it is observed. A well organized content analysis will also take into account representativeness in that thought will go into how media reports should be sampled. If the researcher is interested in how crime is reported in tabloid newspapers, then they might sample the coverage of three newspapers on three days of the week over a period of a month. If the researcher is interested in the impact of television advertising on its audience, they may sample television commercials from different parts of the day over several channels over several weeks. If they are interested in how the media coverage of crime has changed, they might access library archives and sample newspaper coverage of crime across the century or they may focus on past and present high profile criminal trials and their coverage by a variety of newspapers. If the sociologist is interested in how readership is influenced by newspapers or magazines, then they might sample those publications with the largest audiences, although this may not be entirely satisfactory because sales figures tell us very little about the social characteristics of audiences and people are often selective in how they use the media, i.e. in what they watch or read.

Ferguson used this type of content analysis in her study of 1970s' women's magazines. Her hypothesis suggested that such magazines encouraged young women to subscribe to an 'ideology of femininity', i.e. the messages they transmitted promoted being a mother and housewife over other potential options. Ferguson, therefore, needed to operationalize the concept of 'ideology of femininity' into a number of codes or categories that she could count in order to support her hypothesis.

Other feminist sociologists have made content analyses of children's books, to highlight how boys are usually shown in active, creative, practical roles, whereas girls are shown as passive, domestic and as followers rather than leaders. This involves creating a list of categories such as 'takes lead' or 'follows', 'gives orders' or 'obeys orders', 'works out of doors' or 'works indoors', 'mends car' or 'does housework', and counting up each occasion on which the characters in the book do these things. In some traditional reading books there was a clear assumption that boys were leaders and girls were followers. More recently, books have been written which try to avoid these stereotypes

The early research carried out by the Glasgow University Media Group into press and TV coverage of major events relied heavily on this quantitative technique. For example, they videotaped all TV news bulletins in the early months of 1975, and then spent a year analysing the stories into categories such as parliamentary politics, Northern Ireland, terrorism, demonstrations, Labour Party internal, crime, economics (currency), economics (business) and sport. They measured the frequency of particular types of news story and, in particular, examined where they were placed in the overall news schedule in order to uncover patterns of bias. Their research produced statistical evidence of the way in which TV news systematically favoured certain points of view of current events, rather than maintaining the balance that was claimed (Glasgow University Media Group 1976 and 1985).

This type of quantitative content analysis has been used successfully to examine visual culture. Research by Lutz and Collins (1993) examined the representations of non-western cultures in the *National Geographic* magazine. They identified twenty-two characteristics which were coded and applied these to 594 photographs sampled from articles produced between 1950 and 1986. They revealed how the magazine's photographs reflected western assumptions about the lifestyles of people from faraway places, i.e. that they were 'exotic', 'strange', 'primitive', etc.

Formal content analysis has been a popular method because it is relatively straightforward to use. Mass media reports exist in a variety of readily available and accessible forms, and consequently it is fairly cheap to construct a sample and content frame. It is regarded as a reasonably reliable method, especially if a team of researchers is using what Gomm (2004) calls 'inter-rater reliability' when two people independently of each other record and analyse media content using the same content frames and codes. Results can then be compared, differences between them discussed, and codes and frames modified so that all researchers understand precisely what constitutes a particular category or code. It is also deemed attractive because it is a non-reactive and unobtrusive method, i.e. the document is not affected by the fact that you are using it nor is any human sample directly involved in the research.

However, formal content analysis is seen to have some limitations. First, the coding method may not be very reliable because it is the end product of personal interpretation, whether it is an individual or team effort. Such interpretation may be unconsciously influenced by the political and ideological values of the researchers and, consequently, biased. Other teams of researchers might classify data quite differently. Second, if researchers look hard enough for something, there is a likelihood that they will find it, especially if what they are looking at is taken out of context of the overall media report and reduced to a set of statistics. Third, analysing media reports tells us very little about the effect on audiences – we may find evidence of what we are looking for but that is no guarantee that audiences are taking any notice of it. It is necessary, therefore, to use content analysis in conjunction with other methods which focus on the audience, e.g. some studies have asked people to author news stories themselves and compared these with those that appear in the newspaper or newscast. Fourth, it is argued that a statistical analysis cannot reveal the subtlety of media messages and uncover meanings which may not be literal or on the surface. Sociologists using formal content analysis may therefore miss the significance and underlying meaning of the text. Finally, content analysis ignores questions about why the media report was produced and presented in the way that it was in the first place.

The influence of semiotics

In the last twenty years, sociological researchers studying the media have adopted more qualitative versions of content analysis. These have been influenced by the academic discipline of semiotics, i.e. the scientific study of signs or codes. It was argued that signs and symbols underpin all forms of behaviour and language. Consequently, they are part and parcel of culture and their meaning is learnt and communicated through socialization.

In terms of media texts, semiotics aims to uncover the hidden meanings that lay behind the use of particular words or images. Signs are said to be made up of two parts; the signifier or denotation and the signified or connotation. The signifier is quite simply what we can see or hear, whereas the signified is its meaning, i.e. what it symbolizes. Semiotics note that objects often represent things other than themselves. For example, the signifier 'house' denotes a property in which people live but it also has a range of symbolic or connotative meanings, including 'home', 'family', 'security', 'financial investment', etc. Those who employ semiotic analysis believe that it can be employed successfully in regard to the sociological analysis of text and visual images included in media reports.

Textual analysis

Pawson (1999) notes that textual analysis involves analysing the linguistic subtleties within documents in order to see whether they encourage a particular interpretation of events. The use of textual analysis has been common in sociological analysis of documents since the 1960s. Cohen's (1987) study of the mods and rockers conflicts in the mid-1960s looked closely at the reporting of particular incidents and noted a media propensity to exaggerate the meaning of youth conflict through the use of words such as 'battle', 'riot' and 'crisis'. However, the Glasgow University Media Group (1976, 1985) were probably the first research group to formally employ semiotics in textual and visual analysis in their study of the way that industrial disputes were reported on the television. They observed that journalists often talked about strikers making 'demands' whilst management made 'offers' or 'proposals' which were often 'rejected' by workers. The visual images used by news broadcasts confirmed this 'aggressive worker' versus 'passive/reasonable management' stance constructed by the media by interviewing workers in situations which confirmed the text, e.g. on the picket line with all its associated hustle and bustle and by showing images of the inconvenience 'caused' by the strike, etc. In contrast, management were interviewed in the calm environment of their offices and very rarely called upon to justify their actions.

Thematic analysis

Pawson identifies a second type of semiotic analysis: thematic analysis, which attempts to identify ideological themes which may underpin news stories. Sometimes, these are quite obvious from the political stance of the newspaper in which the news item originates. In the UK, newspapers openly align themselves with political parties. For example, a political story appearing in the Conservative Party-supporting *Daily Mail* will probably have a different emphasis to a story appearing in the *Daily Mirror* which has traditionally supported the Labour Party. However, ideological biases are often more subtle and complex and, consequently, less visible and may only be uncovered by using semiotic analysis.

Marvasti (2004) focuses on how sociologists might use still photos, videos, cinematic images and television programmes to document and analyse social life. He refers to this as 'visual sociology'. He argues that western culture has become a visual culture because of the dominance of television and advertising. Rose (2001) goes further and suggests that the status of the visual has overtaken the written word. He argues that today images dominate how we see particular issues. Using a semiotic thematic analysis, he argues that magazine covers featuring attractive girls want the audience to see females as objects to be admired for their physical beauty and this tells us a great deal about women's place in western society.

Denzin (1995) argues that cultures understand and express themselves and their social settings through Hollywood films. He suggests that movies do more than simply entertain – rather, they provide cultural guides on how members of society should relate to each other. Denzin's sociological analysis of films such as *When Harry Met Sally* shows how cinematic images both construct and validate our experience of cultural norms, e.g. how men and women in western societies are supposed to relate to one another.

The critique of semiotics

Critics of semiotic-based research argue that semiotics lack methodological rigour – in particular, it is seen to lack both reliability and objectivity because there are few methodological guidelines for practising semiotics. The method is very reliant on the researcher's subjective and often selective interpretation of the text or image and this raises questions about its validity, i.e. it may be at odds with the interpretations of other researchers and the audience. Moreover, it is very doubtful whether such research can be replicated. It tells us little about why the text was created in the way it was or about the effect on the audience. Even supporters of semiotic-based research acknowledge that it is less concerned with detached scientific objectivity and more concerned with uncovering social inequalities and explaining how these are rationalized through visual imagery. However, it remains an attractive methodological option because it can be used in conjunction with formal content analysis and interviews with members of audiences can be used to test the validity of sociological and semiotic interpretations of media content.

The internet

The use of the internet as a source of information about the social world by researchers, teachers and students has increased dramatically in the last decade. Lee (2000) notes that the internet has great potential as an information source for sociologists. Information produced and classified by someone else can easily be retrieved even when the data is located at a site thousands of miles away. Moreover, the internet's democratic character, i.e. the fact that anyone can post something up on their own web-site, means that data does not always have to be the product of some powerful academic elite – the world-wide web is potentially more representative than traditionally produced academic texts and research (although it could be equally argued that it is still western-centric and that access to computers, both within western societies in terms of social class and world-wide is still deeply unequal).

Lee notes that the democratic character of the internet also makes the finding of valuable information difficult. However, he argues that search engines are becoming increasingly sophisticated and the development of 'subject gateways' are particularly useful in focusing on only reliable, high content sites. The following social science gateways are accessible and useful to sociology students:

Research Resources for the Social Sciences: http://www.
  socsciresearch.com
Social Sciences Data Collection: http://ssdc.ucsd.edu/
Sociosite: http://www.pscw.uva.nl/sociosite/
Social Science Information Gateway: http://www.sosig.ac.uk

Lee argues that the internet has several advantages for the
sociological researcher. First, it is generally an unobtrusive
method in that sifting through the secondary data found on
the world-wide web does not directly influence or harm human
behaviour in any way. It does not involve the direct inter-
vention of the sociological researcher. Second, the democratic
and diffuse nature of the internet has dramatically expanded
sociological horizons in regard to the sheer volume of potential
data available. Consequently in terms of what sociologists can
find 'serendipity is an ever-present possibility' (Lee 2000:
115). Third, many social activities and relationships which
are difficult to study directly, are recorded and can be traced
on-line. Many illegal and deviant activities are represented on
the internet and in chat-rooms, and consequently researchers
can study how people who subscribe to such activities (by
examining the web-sites and/or going into virtual chat-rooms)
relate to the activity and each other.

However, Stein (2002) urges caution in the use of the
internet as a source of secondary data because its content has
not been academically or scientifically verified and checked for
reliability or accuracy. He argues that a number of criteria need
to be satisfied before material from the web can be used. The
credentials of the author(s) need to be examined in terms of
their qualifications, previous publications and the references
that they cite. The organization which maintains the site needs
to be reputable although this should not be a problem so long
as the researcher is aware of the value position taken by those
who maintain and contribute to the site.

Unobtrusive methods

One of the great strengths of most of the secondary data referred to in this chapter is the fact that it is unobtrusive, i.e. sociological analysis of it very rarely directly intrudes on people's lives. The use of it does not involve direct contact with people. However, some sociologists have attempted to construct research strategies that do not involve analysis of conventional forms of secondary data such as statistics and documents. Nevertheless, what they study is in a sense a form of secondary data because it is composed of the 'traces' left behind by human beings in particular situations. The data is not primary in that it is not the direct result of a sociologist employing a specific research tool.

Webb *et al.* (1966) argue that instead of directly addressing people, either through interviewing or participant observation, we should instead devote sociological attention to examining physical traces that people leave behind them as they go about their daily lives. Robson (2002) notes that human beings produce 'artefacts' or by-products that can be studied by sociologists in order to understand the lifestyle of particular cultures without having to come into direct contact with them.

Robson notes two broad types of unobtrusive measures which can produce secondary data that the sociologist can 'read' and analyse.

Accretion measures   An accretion is something extra or added to a social environment such as litter or graffiti. A sociologist interested in racism might examine the frequency and nature of racist graffiti in a particular neighbourhood. For example, they might conclude that racism is related to football in some sense if racist graffiti appears more frequently near football grounds and/or alongside graffiti celebrating a football team. A sociologist investigating the role of religion might examine the number of hits on the web-sites of a range of churches whereas observations might be made about people's eating and drinking habits from examining the contents of their dustbins. Dethlefsen (1981) has examined cemeteries because he believes that they reflect the living community around them. The way they are maintained and, in particular, the inscriptions on gravestones can offer insights into how the community views death and the spiritual/religious realm. For example, his study of four cemeteries in Florida serving different types of communities concluded attitudes towards family life had changed radically over a period of fifty years.

Erosion measures   Erosion refers to deterioration or wear. A sociologist interested in the popularity of certain exhibits in a museum or art gallery might look at the wear and tear of the floor in front of the exhibit to assess this. Ley and Cybriwsky (1974) used an erosion measure to examine the relationship between surveillance and delinquency. Their hypothesis suggested that delinquency as indicated by the stripping of abandoned cars was more likely to be carried out in spaces in which residents exerted little control. They found all the abandoned cars in one inner city neighbourhood and found that those which were stripped were more likely to be found on land that encouraged criminal activity because it was difficult to observe behaviour there.

Box 5.1   A variety of unobtrusive measures

- the diameter of a circle of children as an index of fear induced by a ghost-story-telling session;
- degree of clustering of white, Asian and African-Caribbean students in a college social area;
- settings of car radios when brought into a garage for service as an index of the relative popularity of different stations;
- amount of graffiti in pairs of male and female public toilets as an index of gender differences;
- number of times books are borrowed from a library (or bought from bookshops) as indices of popularity.

(Adapted from Robson 2002: 348)

Unobtrusive methods are, therefore, attractive because they do not have a direct or indirect effect upon those being investigated. However, they are not without difficulties. Robson notes that it may be impossible to identify the person(s) responsible for the trace or to assess the contribution of the research population, e.g. some people may over-contribute because they are more heavily involved in a particular activity. Moreover, you can never be sure that the trace has not been contaminated by natural factors. For example, counting the number of people going through a turnstile may have more to do with the weather than the popularity of an event. Finally, some ethical concerns are raised by the nature of some of this research. For example, does going through someone's dustbin require consent? It might be that people's rubbish reveals aspects of their life that they might prefer to keep hidden. However, despite these problems, there may be room for the use of ingenious unobtrusive measures alongside more traditional methods as part of a triangulation approach to a particular sociological problem.

6

Science and values

This chapter is not concerned so much with how research is done, but rather with some of the more abstract arguments surrounding sociological research, especially the relationship sociology has with science.

Science and sociology

During the eighteenth and nineteenth centuries, science replaced religion as the major source of knowledge in western societies. No longer did people automatically look to the Church for the answers to questions about the world. Rather as Woodward and Watt (2000) argue 'empirical, rational science usurped the authoritative status of appeals to the divine and the tradition of religion'. The elevation of science to the most dominant belief system in western society in this period was based on a succession of important scientific discoveries, specifically, the development of machine technology, and the achievements of Victorian civil and mechanical engineers. Great advances were made in food technology, e.g. freezing and canning, public health and medicine which had remarkable consequences for the health and general living standards of most of the population. It, therefore, seemed clear to the leading thinkers in this period that there was a body of knowledge that existed independently of whether people knew it or not, and that the task of the scientist was to uncover that knowledge piece by piece, building up a more complete understanding of the laws of nature.

Sociology first appeared as a distinctive academic discipline in the nineteenth century when science was probably at its most influential. We should not be too surprised that the early sociologists were impressed by the status of science and scientists, and consequently that they adopted the philosophical principles that underpinned the scientific approach, as well as borrowing many scientific techniques of data collection.

Such ideas particularly appealed to nineteenth-century theorists such as Comte, Durkheim and Marx who already were arguing in their own distinctive ways that society was more important than the individual and that we needed to examine the organization of society, i.e. its social and economic structure, if we were to understand human behaviour. These sociologists believed that only scientific enquiry could provide objective knowledge which was true in all circumstances. They claimed that sociology, too, could be scientific if sociological research based itself on the methods and logic of the natural sciences and aimed to uncover the scientific or social 'laws' that underpinned the organization of society and thus all social behaviour. Comte, in particular, argued that adopting the methods of the natural sciences would result in a 'positive science of society'. Moreover, he believed that such knowledge could be used to predict human behaviour (and therefore the future of society) and consequently social scientists could engage in social engineering and solve many of society's problems such as crime and deviance. Sociologists who enthusiastically adopted this positivist approach were quick to brand themselves 'social scientists'.

The nineteenth century, then, saw the enthusiastic embrace of science by the so-called classical sociologists; but differences soon emerged over what type of science sociologists should be adopting and what precisely should be the focus of social science investigation. For example, Comte, Durkheim and Marx argued that the level of scientific analysis should be the social structure of society, whilst others, most notably, Weber, argued that it should be focused on the individual and social action. Some, mainly functionalist sociologists, argued that scientific research should focus on explaining the social order that they saw characterizing modern societies whilst others, mainly Marxist sociologists, argued that it should focus on exploring the conflict that they saw simmering beneath the surface of capitalist societies. However, the fundamental difference that existed between sociologists in the twentieth century focused on the question, 'what is meant by "science" or the "scientific method"?'

Robson (2002) notes that the positivist view of what science is contains a number of assumptions. First, it assumes that objective knowledge can only be gained from direct experience or observation. Things that are invisible or theoretical are rejected as subjects of scientific investigation because they cannot be observed or directly experienced. Second, science is 'value-free', i.e. it is only by being an objective or detached observer that the scientist can prevent the contamination of data by subjective influences such as emotions and prejudices. This definition of science therefore places the scientist on a pedestal – he or she is portrayed as a white-coated, incorruptible individual whose sole motivation is to seek and find the holy grail of scientific truth. As Lawson (1993) notes 'neither institution nor personal consideration, neither threat nor bribe, can deflect this exemplary person from the quest for objective knowledge'. Third, science is seen as largely based on the collection of quantitative and factual evidence resulting from the application of logical and systematic procedures. This is what separates science from common sense or journalism. The hypothetico-deductive approach outlined and illustrated in diagrammatic form on p. 69 is the most typical form that this logical and systematic procedure takes. Fourth, the purpose of science is to uncover relationships between events or variables in order to develop universal causal laws. In order for this to happen, the conditions of the observation or experiment must be strictly controlled, usually in a laboratory context.

The foundation stone on which most science rests is 'induction', this is essentially replication, i.e. repeating the experiment or observation. If the data collected is the same time and time again, then both the information collected and the conclusions reached on the basis of that data, are reliable. As Lawson notes, it is only when the results obtained are identical that other scientists are satisfied that 'truth' has been achieved.

Positivism, science and sociology

If we examine the world of sociological research, we can see that positivist ideas about what science is and how it ought to be conducted have had a significant influence on sociological methods and procedures.

Sociological positivists argue that sociological research methods should exhibit certain crucial features. Data, ideally of a quantitative sort, must be collected under controlled conditions, i.e. preferably in a logical, systematic and standardized way that can be replicated by other researchers in order to ensure reliability. Moreover, the sociologist should make sure that the research process is characterized by objectivity, i.e. values should not be allowed to bias any aspect of data collection. The final research findings should be generalizable so that laws, even if only partial laws, can be established.

Positivist sociologists, therefore, are happy to highlight the scientific credentials of sociology. The limitations of using the laboratory method for sociological research purposes are acknowledged (see Chapter 3) but positivists argue that the social survey which involves the use of questionnaires and structured interviews, is an ideal scientific tool of sociological investigation. Such surveys are usually controlled through the use of random sampling techniques, pilot surveys and the objective design of value-free questions. They are seen as objective, especially in their questionnaire form, because there is minimal contact between the sociologist and the respondents. They are replicable in that other researchers should be able to distribute the same questionnaire to similar samples and get the same result. Surveys usually produce quantifiable data which can be presented in a number of forms for comparative analysis. Correlations can, therefore, be observed which may form the basis for the establishing of social laws.

Challenging the positivist definition of science

The positivist view of science and scientific method has been subjected to severe criticism over the years and this had a knock-on effect upon the social sciences, and especially the view that sociology is a scientific discipline. Much of this critique has stemmed from the observation that positivist sociological research has not yet produced any 'scientific' laws, despite a century's worth of endeavour. As Robson notes, 'the argument advanced here is that it is the "standard" positivistic scientific view which is wrong: both as providing an account of how natural science takes place, and as a model for the social sciences' (2002: 21).

In the later part of the twentieth century, there was a radical sea-change in the view of what is involved in studying natural science. After the certainties and the optimism of the nineteenth century, science has had a much rougher ride in recent years. We are now more aware of the possible abuse of scientific knowledge, and of the sometimes disastrous side-effects of the things that are done to the environment in the name of scientific progress. We know that scientists have sometimes been wrong, and this knowledge has led to some loss of status for natural science.

Philosophers of science have also questioned the accounts of how natural science research is done. Rose (1998) notes that positivist scientists have generally been concerned with proving rather than disproving hypotheses. Most accept that they cannot prove absolute certainty but the emphasis of their research has been more geared to looking for evidence that confirms their ideas than looking for evidence that proves them absolutely wrong and forces them to look elsewhere. Karl Popper (1934) argued that the logic of the hypothetico-deductive model, i.e. its emphasis on the positive, was wrong. Popper claimed that there is no such thing as 'objective truth' which can be discovered and documented. At best, we can only achieve partial truth because all knowledge is provisional or temporary. This is because no matter how many times an experiment is conducted or a phenomena is observed, the scientist can never be certain that the same results will always be obtained in the future.

Popper illustrated this idea by using the hypothesis 'all swans are white'. He noted that many scientists would be content to confirm this hypothesis after 999 observations of white swans. The notion that 'all swans are white' would become a scientific fact and it is unlikely that further observations would be carried out. However, Popper noted that this is bad science because there is always the possibility that a black swan will appear and prove this 'fact' wrong. In other words, Popper argued that we can never be conclusively right, we can only be conclusively wrong. No amount of evidence in support of an hypothesis can ever prove that hypothesis whereas a single piece of evidence that contradicts the hypothesis proves it wrong. In regard to Popper's swan example, all the scientist can say with any confidence is 'the swans observed so far are white'.

Popper argued that good science is about being rigorously sceptical and he proposed that scientific research methods should be based on the 'principle of falsification', i.e. instead of looking for evidence to prove a hypothesis right, scientists should look for evidence that proves it false. As Woodward and Watt (2000) note

> Popper requires scientists to be fundamentally sceptical; to be detached enough observers who are capable of rejecting theories when the evidence is against them, even when they strongly believe in these theories. In effect, it requires scientists to be suspicious of their common-sense intuitions.
>
> (p. 21)

Moreover, Popper argued that scientific knowledge is that which survives after rigorous testing – it can be tentatively accepted as close to the truth but it is possible that, one day, contradictory evidence will appear and deny it the status of real scientific truth.

Popper was sceptical about the scientific status of sociology because he argued that it was too theoretical and not engaged in enough testing. However, although this was probably true at the time Popper was writing, modern sociology has engaged extensively in the research process in ways that stress that nothing should ever taken on trust and that evidence should be subjected to the most rigorous critical examination.

Paul Feyerabend (1978) was critical of both positivists and Popper because both portray scientific method as being a coldly logical process, proceeding step by step in a rational manner. It appears to generate more and more knowledge, gradually increasing the total of human understanding of the natural world, which is there, waiting to be understood and explained. In contrast, Feyerabend suggested that what scientists say they do is often quite different from what they actually do. He claims that there is no such thing as a scientific method good for all times and in all places, whether it be the positivist hypothetico-deductive process or Popper's falsification procedure. In fact, Feyerabend argued that there is no logic to science – the rule seems to be 'anything goes' – individual scientists follow their own rules, and these often do not resemble the textbook models.

Kaplan had come to the same conclusions as Feyerabend. He pointed out that many scientific discoveries are made almost by accident, and that inspired guesses, imagination, and luck all play a crucial role in scientific research. Moreover, many scientists make false starts or collect data that takes them up blind alleys before they get back on track. Kaplan noted that when scientists write up their accounts of the research process in scientific journals, they 'reconstruct logic', i.e. their account focuses on what they thought should have happened and what fellow scientists expect to read rather than the haphazard reality. Moreover, some critics have questioned the central role of induction in the scientific process by pointing out that few research findings are verified by other scientists replicating experiments because there is little prestige in redoing someone else's work.

Feyerabend argued that the gap between the reality of the research process and the official version leads to the mystification of scientific knowledge, i.e. the view that science is beyond the understanding and reach of most ordinary people and therefore scientists deserve greater status and rewards because only they understand the logic of scientific enquiry.

Scientific realism

Scientific realists argue that positivists are mistaken about the nature of science. They note that not all natural sciences insist on controlling variables or observing phenomena. Many sciences, which Sayer (2000) refers to as 'open sciences' theorize about the existence of phenomena which are either difficult or impossible to observe, detect and consequently predict. For example, seismology, meteorology, astronomy and some schools of physics are open sciences that are concerned with the study of things we cannot see or sense directly. However, realism claims that there is a reality that exists independently of our awareness of it and therefore the invisible 'things' studied by open sciences such as gravity, protons, black holes, sub-atomic particles and evolution, actually exist. Moreover, realists accept that such open sciences are often unable to predict how the phenomena they are studying are going to behave. For example, seismologists cannot predict precisely when and where an earthquake is going to occur. Controlling variables, then, is virtually impossible.

Realists argue that the definition of science employed by positivism is inadequate because of its emphasis on control and observable cause. Instead realists see science as an attempt to explain the effects of underlying and often unobservable structures and processes. For example, earthquakes are explained in terms of the movement of phenomena known as 'tectonic plates' which have never been directly observed by seismologists. Realists reject the positivist view that theories are in need of constant testing and that observations are the foundation of such tests – rather realists argue that observations are tenuous and may be in need of regular reinterpretation, whereas theories are not hypothetical but, instead, very real.

From a realist position, sociology can be seen as scientific because it is largely concerned with developing models of underlying social structures and processes which are largely unobservable but which can be evaluated and modified by examining their effects. For example, social class as a social and economic force cannot be directly observed but its effects upon social behaviour can be measured. In this sense, then, sociology could be classed as an open science.

Science and paradigms

Thomas Kuhn (1970) took this debate about what science is in another direction. He argued that scientists are not as open-minded as positivists claim. He rejected the idea that scientists are constantly making and testing hypotheses. Rather, he argued, they are mainly concerned with solving problems defined as important by earlier influential scientists. In other words, scientists normally work within a set of assumptions about what the natural world is like that have been left by an earlier generation of scientists. These are not questioned, but are taken for granted as correct. He called these sets of assumptions 'paradigms' and argued that these shape and define what goes on within normal science. Within any one science, the paradigm shapes the scientists' view of the world – it tells them what their priorities should be, what counts as legitimate evidence and how particular problems should be approached. In short, it advises them what scientific method should be adopted.

We can illustrate the concept of paradigms with an historical example. The dominant paradigm in early astronomy was developed by the priest-scientists within the Roman Catholic Church; it stated that the earth was the centre of the universe, and that the sun revolved around it. This set of assumptions or paradigm was so powerful that it was accepted without question. It was not tested and contradictory evidence was ignored. When Galileo presented evidence that challenged this paradigm, i.e. that showed that the earth actually revolved around the sun, he was imprisoned and his data was suppressed.

Kuhn suggested that scientific progress only occurs because as time passes, more and more evidence appears that does not fit the paradigm. At first it is ignored or explained away, but eventually becomes so abundant that the dominant paradigm loses credibility and is overthrown in a 'scientific revolution'. A new paradigm is established, and normal science resumes. We can see a good example of this revolutionary change in the field of physics. Nineteenth-century physics was dominated by a Newtonian paradigm based upon a mechanistic view of the universe. This paradigm was eventually overthrown in the twentieth century and replaced by a new paradigm based upon the ideas of Albert Einstein.

Kuhn challenged the positivist view that science is a method. Rather, Kuhn saw science as a body of knowledge constructed and created by scientists working within a particular paradigmatic context. Scientific method, therefore, is not free to wander in any direction it wishes – it is actually constrained by taken-for-granted assumptions about how the world is organized. Kuhn also showed us that the history of science is not the logical progression celebrated by positivism. He pointed out that scientific knowledge is produced in fits and starts as paradigms begin to conflict and begin a long struggle for dominance.

Overall, then, Kuhn's major contribution to the debate about science is that scientific knowledge does not exist independently and objectively, but is constructed and produced by scientists working within particular paradigms. Objectivity and truth cannot exist in the ideal positivist sense because what scientists research and how they go about it is highly dependent on pre-conceived and sometimes quite false ideas, which for long periods, go unchallenged.

If we accept Kuhn's definition of science as a body of paradigmatic knowledge, sociology is probably not scientific because it is doubtful whether there has ever been one dominant sociological paradigm. Sociology has long been characterized by competing theoretical perspectives and even within these, there is intense disagreement. For example, there are several different types of feminisms and many versions of Marxism. Some sociologists claim that sociology exists in a permanent state of revolution whilst others claim that it is in a pre-paradigmatic state, meaning that a single paradigm has yet to be accepted.

The relativist theory of science

Kuhn's ideas are closely related to the relativist or social constructionist view of scientific knowledge. The central theme of this position is that all knowledge is a product of its social context, and will therefore vary from one context to another. It is produced rather than discovered. This is easy to accept when we are talking about history or literature, but some would argue that natural science is essentially no different from these other forms of knowledge.

The familiar word 'data' illustrates the point. 'Data' means, literally, 'things that are given', i.e. there, waiting to be found. It assumes a positivist view of the world. But if knowledge is created and constructed, then data is not 'given', but produced. We need a different word, which stresses how knowledge is a product, not a given. Every research method is a means of *producing* knowledge, not *collecting* it. None simply records 'the facts' or 'the truth' as an external object.

Relativists argue that scientific knowledge has achieved a higher status than other forms of knowledge because it is the product of powerful groups who have used such knowledge to maintain and legitimate inequality. In this sense, then, science cannot be objective or value-free. Barnes *et al.* (1996) argue that powerful capitalist interests define what counts as science in western societies. Interests such as big business and especially the military define what science needs to be done and how it should be done. For example, Sklair (1991) argues that science has been geared to improving worker productivity and enhancing profit because it has largely focused on developing technological advances in assembly-line production, computers and robots. Low priority has been accorded to the job satisfaction or health and safety of workers. Similarly, Baird (1988) notes how medical research has focused on profit-making drugs and how little attention has been paid to developing drugs which might alleviate disease in developing societies or finding substitutes for toxic solvents, asbestos or nuclear power. Moreover, alternative forms of science such as 'green technology' are subjected to abuse and undermined by claims that they lack scientific validity because they potentially threaten the monopoly of profit-driven science.

Feminists, too, have taken a relativist position on science and knowledge. They point out that the female contribution to science is often devalued and made invisible, thus giving the impression that science can only be mastered by males using skills that come 'naturally' to them such as logic and rationality. Moreover, they note that knowledge, including sociological knowledge, has been used by men as an ideology to justify gender inequality and to accord low status to women's interests. It can be argued that much scientific research, some of which has had a profound influence on sociological thinking, e.g. sociobiology, has been geared to 'proving' that women are inferior to men.

Interpretivism and science

The revival of interpretative and phenomenological perspectives in sociology, which stressed the difference, first emphasized by Weber, between the subject matter of natural science and that of social science led to a fundamental attack on positivist ideas about science. Interpretivist sociology is sceptical about positivist sociology's claim to scientific status and has generally taken an anti-positivist position. Sociologists working within this field argue that the logic and methods of the natural sciences are inappropriate for sociology because the subject matter of sociology, i.e. humans, are active conscious beings, who are aware of what is going on around them and who are constantly making choices about how to act and react. Natural phenomena, on the other hand, lack this ability.

Interpretivists reject the positivist notion that society is the product of social laws and therefore scientific procedures are needed to uncover these. Interpretivists argue that the focus of sociological research should be the interpretations or meanings that people bring to the social interactions that make up society. They argue for the adoption of research methods that help reveal the meanings that lie behind everyday social action. They particularly advocate the use of qualitative ethnographic methods (see Chapter 4) because these focus on people in their everyday natural context and place emphasis upon validity, i.e. taking proper account of the experience and world-view of those being studied. Positivist scientific methods are criticized and rejected by interpretivists because they inevitably result in the sociologist's views of the world being imposed on the research subjects.

Interpretivist sociologists do not reject scientific principles altogether. They argue that reliability can still be achieved but in different ways to those proposed by positivists. For example, observation data can be verified by checking and re-checking what has been observed and supplementing observations with informal conversations with those being studied. Many observers, too, use observation schedules that permit the gathering of quantitative data. Interpretivists also stress the importance of researcher reflexivity, i.e. a form of critical self-appraisal using devices such as research diaries to identify problems in the research process and to explain how these were solved (see p. 116).

Postmodernism and science

Postmodernists reject the view that there exists any absolute and universal truth and knowledge, and consequently reject science as an embodiment of this position. Many postmodernist accounts of science are critical of the relationship between it and capitalism. In particular, science is criticized because it has not been put to use for universal good, rather it has been used as a tool of western exploitation in its development of industrial technology and weapons of mass destruction. They also draw attention to the legacy of science in terms of pollution, environmental destruction and human suffering.

Postmodernists are particularly critical of science because it claims to be objective. Like relativists, postmodernists argue that scientific knowledge is a social production that reflects the values of powerful western interest groups. The rules of science such as logic and rationality are merely ways in which the powerful attempt to control ways of thinking.

Postmodernists argue that scientific truth and certainty are illusions constructed by western academics. They argue that science has no more authority than any other subjective version of events and therefore traditional hard science approaches that insist on facts and truth should be abandoned in favour of a more speculative science in the context of an uncertain and unpredictable world.

Postmodernism has implications for sociological research. First, it argues that sociology should abandon its search for grand truth, whether this be the factual truth sought by methodological disciplines such as positivism or the philosophical truth sought by theories (or meta-narratives, as postmodernists call them) such as Marxism, functionalism, etc. Second, postmodernists advocate a more varied approach to scientific enquiry so that a range of research tools can be employed to capture and analyse the many different interpretations of reality that are thought to characterize postmodern society.

Science: some conclusions

Whether or not sociology is a science depends on what is meant by science. The best answer to this is to see science as a method rather than a body of knowledge. What distinguishes both social and natural science from non-science, from common sense and from ideology, is method. Good sociology is logically derived from empirical evidence. The evidence, and how it was collected, are made available to others who can check the conclusions that have been drawn. Sociologists are not the only people capable of producing insights into how the social world operates, but they have been trained in a rigorous and critical way of thinking, which demands that nothing is ever taken on trust but is always subjected to critical examination in the light of all the evidence available. Sociologists are usually their own strongest critics, and these internal disputes are sometimes seen as a sign of the weakness of the discipline. They are not weaknesses, but strengths, in a discipline that is rooted in critical analysis.

Many modern sociologists are happy to open up their research process to public scrutiny in order to validate their methodological rigour. Most original studies now include a frank reflexive account of the trials and tribulations of the research, including a statement about the researcher's own background, since this is acknowledged to have an important bearing on the validity and the reliability of the research. Many of these research studies highlight their own methodological weaknesses and explain in detail how verification and validity were achieved. Such accounts do not necessarily cast doubt on the scientific status of the work done. If the ideal of natural scientific method is in fact a myth, then sociologists cannot be criticized for failing to match up to it. Instead, we have to revise our view of what science is.

Some sociologists such as Bryman (1988) argue that the so-called incompatibility between scientific and non-scientific approaches has been exaggerated. He advocates the use of triangulation which combines elements of both approaches in applied research (see p. 23). Some postmodernist sociologists advocate methodological pluralism (see p. 22). Other sociologists such as Robson recommend pragmatic approaches to sociological enquiry, i.e. 'use whatever philosophical or methodological approach works best for a particular research problem at issue' (2002: 43). For Robson and others like him, truth is what works best – scientific methods and philosophies need not be necessarily incompatible with non-scientific approaches such as interpretivism. Rather such approaches to sociological enquiry are inter-related and sociologists need to use whatever suits their purposes rather than worrying about whether they are betraying any particular position in what has been largely a fantasy theory war.

Values

Nineteenth-century positivist sociologists, as we have seen, believed that their task was to discover the laws of social development in order that a better society could be created. They had no reservations about the idea that their purpose in discovering the 'truth' was to improve things, in whatever field. Comte believed sociology could be the science of society whilst Durkheim believed that sociology could propose remedies for social and moral problems. The early poverty studies of Booth and Rowntree, not only aimed to describe the extent of poverty, but to also propose policies for its eradication.

In the twentieth century, however, developments in positivism led to the belief that facts could and should be separated from values. The view that the scientist's task is to document social phenomena in an objective fashion and identify scientific laws, and that is all, became extremely influential. It was seen as the role of the policy makers to act upon sociological findings. The notion of a search for objective and value-free knowledge became identified with a belief that the scientist should be morally indifferent as to how the sociological knowledge they had gathered was used. Social scientists, it was believed, should not aim to change society rather they should subscribe to 'objectivity through neutrality'. They should aim only to see facts as they are, not as they may wish to see them. So, in this period, sociologists were turned into scientists – disinterested and value-free pursuers of 'truth'.

Today, most sociologists accept the position first spelled out by Weber which he called 'value-relevance': choice of topic is inevitably influenced by values, both personal and related to historical context, but such value-commitment should not stretch to the methods used. Science requires that all the evidence should be considered, not just a selection from it, and logical analysis must take precedence over moral convictions. If the results are not what the researcher would have liked them to be, that is just too bad. However, this position rests on the supposition that the sociologist is the only influence on the research process. We have already seen in chapter 1 that sociological research might be influenced by those with power making value judgements about what is worth funding. Some sociologists, dependent upon government funding for their livelihoods (after all, they, too, have mortgages to pay), may avoid being overly-critical of existing social policies or adjust their findings to fit in with dominant thinking on particular issues. Governments and other powerful interests may take only a selective interest in research findings, i.e.

defining data as only interesting and worthwhile if it fits their ideological position on a particular issue or problem.

Some sociologists argue that sociology lacks the means and methods to avoid subjective value judgements because data collection is in itself a social process. We can expect bias and problems of validity to arise out of the interaction between the researcher and subject of research. Many research methods are artificial value-laden devices that provoke artificial responses from their subjects. Those who fill in questionnaires or who are subjected to interviews may feel threatened in a variety of ways by such methods and respond in ways that invalidate the data collected, i.e. they may lie, exaggerate, aim to please, etc. Also, devices such as questionnaires, through the choice of questions and fixed responses, impose what the researcher thinks is important on the research subjects. The research subjects are therefore responding to the values of the sociologist, rather than naturalistically expressing their own values and experiences.

Those who believe that there is no objectively existing truth, independent of its context, such as relativists and post-modernists will argue that any claim to value-free knowledge is a nonsense. A more widely held view is that there can be value-free truth, but that this still leaves the question: 'At what points in the research process is it permissible for values to play a part, and at what points should they be controlled or eliminated?'

This takes us back to the question, 'What is sociology for?' Some sociologists maintain that the task of sociology is just to increase our understanding of social life:

> It may be the case that if we can increase our understanding of a social problem, then we put ourselves in a better position to do something about it. But in doing something about it, we are no longer operating as sociologists, as students of social life: we are operating as social reformers, as politicians, or as citizens. As sociologists, all we can do is to study social life as carefully and as competently as we can.
>
> (Cuff and Payne 1984)

However, Gomm (2004) argues that sociology is socially organized knowledge characterized by collective social attitudes, moral codes, values, prejudices and bias. Sociology cannot avoid values – it is composed of them because sociologists are members of society and therefore cannot escape the influence of its culture and institutions. Gouldner (1973) notes that it is impossible to separate sociologists from what they observe because all researchers possess 'domain assumptions' – a world-view which is the result of their socialization into a particular culture. (This idea is, of course, very similar to Kuhn's idea of paradigms.) What this means is that a great deal of sociological research and theory is not as objective as it claims. Rather it reflects particular values. For example, much educational research on working-class and ethnic minority underachievement often comes at this problem from a middle-class white perspective in its criticisms of parental values and practices. In this sense, then, sociological research may reflect ideological beliefs about the world which are held by powerful interests. Sociological explanations such as those that argue that poverty is the result of the individual or culture rather than the way society is organized, or that developing countries lack the right sorts of values and institutions to modernize, support particular political positions. Feminists have long complained of the 'malestream' bias of much of the sociology of crime and deviance, and the family.

Gomm (2004) suggests that, by presenting facts as 'truth', sociologists who believe in a value-free sociology can avoid taking responsibility for the way that their research is used by policy-makers. A good deal of sociological research on crime and educational achievement has led to greater controls on working-class and black youth. Moreover, such research has probably distracted from other possible causes of social problems that powerful interests would prefer to ignore such as the social and economic inequalities that derive from the organization of capitalism. Gouldner (1973) wrote of this 'myth of a value-free sociology'. He maintains that this myth has enabled sociologists to evade the moral implications of the work they do, and to avoid offending the powers-that-be. Moral indifference is, he affirms, a deeply immoral stance to take up.

There are sociologists who would argue that, since it is inevitable that values affect the work we do, the important thing is to be clear about what those values are. Becker (1967) posed this question as, 'Whose side are we on?' Becker's answer to this question was that sociologists should not be on anyone's side. He stressed the importance of adopting research that was value-free but he noted that sociologists suffer from the occupational problem that whatever sociologists say it is likely to be seen as being biased in favour of a particular group. Becker's own research is a good example of this. Most writers have seen his classic study, *Outsiders* (1963), as advocating that sociologists should take the side of the 'underdog' against the 'establishment'. However, Gomm argues that the view that Becker was taking the side of the underdog and giving a voice to those who are seldom heard or never heard in public debate ironically largely stems from his insistence on taking a value-free research approach. Becker refused to approach deviance as a social problem (as defined by the powerful) and instead treated it as a sociological puzzle. His central research question deviated from traditional approaches which were asking 'why do people commit deviance and how can we stop them?' The reality, says Gomm, was that Becker was asking the more neutral question 'why is it that some people find the behaviour of other people so objectionable that they try to stop them doing it?' Gomm points out that the answer to this question, despite being collected in an objective way, was seen as more threatening to the establishment who had devised the rules that were being broken. Thus Becker's work was viewed as subversive, biased and taking the side of the underdog.

This leads to a more radical view, which says that it is not enough merely to help people have their say. This does not change their situation. What is needed is a sociology that will show people who are oppressed how to throw off their oppressors. It should be a committed sociology, whose intention is radical or revolutionary change in society, and a fundamental change in power structures. A good deal of Marxist and feminist research adopts this stance. It believes that sociology should not and cannot be morally neutral or indifferent. Rather it should suggest ways forward in order to create a better society.

Such ideas do not necessarily mean that such research is going to be biased or any less scientific than more positivist forms of research. Gomm points out that in the natural sciences, doctors and scientists are often motivated by a sense of social justice and emotional commitment to the health of their patients but this does not prevent them from objectively investigating the causes of poor health. Likewise, radical sociologists may be committed to a particular value position but this should not prevent them from putting aside their values when it comes to designing and applying research in the real world.

Conclusions

It is our view that sociology does not and cannot provide final answers and ultimate truths about the social world, for they do not exist. Sociology is a way of looking at the world that tries to develop new insights by approaching familiar questions from an unfamiliar angle. There is no single reality waiting to be discovered, no one right answer waiting to be found. The test of sociology is how far it helps us to understand the social world, for understanding and knowledge are the foundations of effective action. It will be more successful in doing this if research is done according to principles of integrity and rationality. Choice of topic to study will be value-relevant, but methods must avoid all personal bias and in this sense should be value-free. The use to which any knowledge is put is a profoundly moral issue which sociologists, like other scientists, must not evade.

References

Abrams, P. and McCulloch, A. (1976) *Communes, Sociology and Society*. Cambridge: Cambridge University Press.

Adams, C. (2000) 'Suspect data: arresting research', in R.D. King and E. Wincup (eds) *Doing Research on Crime and Justice*. Oxford: Oxford University Press.

Adler, P. (1985) *Wheeling and Dealing: an Ethnography of an Upper-Level Dealing and Smuggling Community*, new edition, 1993. Washington, DC: Columbia University Press.

Aggleton, P. (1990) *Health*. London: Tavistock.

Anderson, M. (1980) *Approaches to the History of the Western Family 1500–1914*. London: Macmillan.

Armstrong, G. (1998) *Football Hooliganism: Knowing the Score*. Oxford: Berg.

Atkinson, J.M. (1978) *Discovering Suicide: Studies in the Social Organization of Sudden Death*. London: Macmillan.

Atkinson, M. (1984) *Our Masters' Voices: The Language and Body Language of Politics*. London: Methuen.

Atkinson, M.W., Kessel, N. and Dalgaard, J.B. (1975) 'The comparability of suicide rates', *British Journal of Psychiatry* 127: 247–56.

Baird, V. (1988) 'Our future in their hands: methods madness and science', *New Internationalist*, April: 4–6.

Baldwin, J. and McConville, M. (1979) *Jury Trials*. Oxford: Clarendon Press.

Barker, E. (1984) *The Making of a Moonie: Brainwashing or Choice?* Oxford: Blackwell.

Barnes, B., Bloor, D. and Henry, J. (1996) *Scientific Knowledge: A Sociological Analysis*. Chicago: University of Chicago Press.

Barton, E.M., Baltes, M.M. and Orzech, M.J. (1980) 'Etiology of dependence in older nursing home residents during morning care: the role of staff behaviors', *Journal of Personality and Social Psychology* 38: 423–31.

Becker, H.S. (1963) *Outsiders: Studies in the Sociology of Deviance*. New York: The Free Press.

Becker, H.S. (1967) 'Whose side are we on?' *Social Problems* 14.

Becker, H.S., Geer, B., Hughes, E.C. and Strauss, A.L. (1961) *Boys in White*. Chicago: University of Chicago Press.

Becker, H.S., Geer, B. and Hughes, E.G. (1968) *Making the Grade*. New York: Wiley.

Bell, C. and Newby, H. (1971) *Community Studies*. London: Allen & Unwin.

Bell, C. and Newby, H. (1977) *Doing Sociological Research*. London: Allen & Unwin.

Bell, C. and Roberts, H. (1984) *Social Researching*. London: Routledge & Kegan Paul.

Bell, J. (2000) *Doing Your Research Project: A Guide for First-Time Researchers in Education and Social Science*, 3rd edn. Buckingham: Open University Press.

Benson, S. (1981) *Ambiguous Ethnicity: Interracial Families in London*. Cambridge: Cambridge University Press.

Berger, P. and Luckmann, T. (1967) *The Social Construction of Reality*. Harmondsworth: Penguin.

Berman, H.J. (1995) 'Claire Phillip's Journal: from life to text, from text to life', *Journal of Ageing Studies* 9: 335–42.

Best, L. (1993) 'Dragons, dinner ladies and ferrets: sex roles in children's books', *Sociology Review* 2(3), February.

Bhatti, G. (1999) *Asian Children at Home and at School*. London: Routledge.

Bosk. C. (1979) *Forgive and Remember: Managing Medical Failure*. Chicago: University of Chicago Press.

Bott, E. (1971) *Family and Social Network*. London: Tavistock.

Bourgois, P. (1995) *In Search of Respect*. Cambridge: Cambridge University Press.

Box, S. (1987) *Recession, Crime and Punishment*. London: Macmillan.

Brewer, J.D. (1984) *Mosley's Men: The BUF in the West Midlands*. Aldershot: Gower.

Brewer, J.D. (1990) 'Sensitivity as a problem in field research', *American Behavioural Scientist* 33: 578–93.

Brewer, J.D. (1991) *Inside the RUC: Routine Policing in a Divided Society*. Oxford: Clarendon Press.

Brewer, J.D. (2000) *Ethnography*. Buckingham: Open University Press.

Brierley, P. (2003) *Turning the Tide*. London: Christian Research.

Brown, C. and Gay, P. (1985) *Racial Discrimination: 17 Years After the Act*. London: Policy Studies Institute.

Bryman, A. (1988) *Quantity and Quality in Social Research*. London: Allen & Unwin.

Buckingham, D. (1996) *Moving Images*. Manchester: Manchester University Press.

Burgess, R.G. (1983) *Experiencing Comprehensive Education*. London: Methuen.

Burgess, R.G. (1984) *The Research Process in Educational Settings*. Lewes: Falmer.

Calvey, D. (2000) 'Getting on the door and staying there: a covert participant observation study of bouncers', in G. Lee-Treweek and S. Linkogle (eds) *Danger in the Field*. London: Routledge.

Campbell, A. (1984) *The Girls in the Gang*. Oxford: Blackwell.

Carlen, P. (1983) *Women's Imprisonment: A Study in Social Control*. London: Routledge.

Carlen, P. (1985) *Criminal Women*. Cambridge: Polity Press.

Cicourel, A.V. (1976) *The Social Organization of Juvenile Justice*. London: Heinemann.

Cockcroft, T. (1999) 'Oral history and the cultures of the police', in F. Brookman, L. Noaks and E. Wincup (eds) *Qualitative Research in Criminology*. Aldershot: Ashgate.

Coffield, F., Borrill. C. and Marshall, M. (1986) *Growing Up at the Margins*. Oxford: Oxford University Press.

Cohen, S. (1987) *Folk Devils and Moral Panics*. Oxford: Blackwell.

Cohen, S. and Taylor, L. (1972) *Psychological Survival: The Experience of Long-Term Imprisonment*. Harmondsworth: Penguin.

Corrigan, P. (1979) *Schooling the Smash Street Kids*. London: Macmillan.

Croall, H. (1998) *Crime and Society in Britain*. Harlow: Longman.

Cuff, E.C. and Payne, G.C.F. (1984) *Perspectives in Sociology*. London: Allen & Unwin.

Darlington, Y. (1996) *Moving On: Women's Experiences of Childhood Sexual Abuse and Beyond*. Sydney: The Federation Press

Denzin, N. (1982) 'On the ethics of disguised observation: an exchange', in M.Bulmer (ed.) *Social Research Ethics*. London: Macmillan.

Denzin, N. (1995) *The Cinematic Society: The Voyeur's Gaze*. Thousand Oaks, CA: Sage.

Dethlefsen, E.S. (1981) 'The cemetery and culture change: archeological focus and ethnographic perspective', in R.A. Gould and M.B. Schiffer (eds) *Modern Material Culture: The Archeology of Us*. New York: Academic Press.

DeVault, M. (1990) 'Talking and listening from women's standpoint: feminist strategies for interviewing and analysis', *Social Problems* 37(1): 96–116.

Devine, F. (1992) *Affluent Workers Revisited: Privatism and the Working Class*. Edinburgh: Edinburgh University Press.

Devine, F. and Heath, S. (1999) *Sociological Research Methods In Context*. Basingstoke: Macmillan.

Ditton, J. (1977) *Part-Time Crime: An Ethnography of Fiddling and Pilferage*. London: Macmillan.

Dohrenwend, B.P. and Dohrenwend, B.S. (1969) *Social Status and Psychological Disorder*. New York: Wiley.

Douglas, J. (1985) *Creative Interviewing*. London: Sage.

Douglas, J.W.B. (1964) *The Home and the School*. London: MacGibbon & Kee.

Douglas, J.W.B. (1968) *All Our Future*. London: Peter Davies.

Durkheim, E. (1895) *The Rules of Sociological Method*. London: Collier Macmillan, 1938; New York: The Free Press, 1964.

Durkheim, E. (1897) *Suicide: A Study in Sociology*. London: Routledge & Kegan Paul, 1970.

Dyer, C. (1995) *Beginning Research in Psychology*. Oxford: Blackwell.

Dyson, S. (1987) *Mental Handicap*. London: Croom Helm.

Dyson, S. (1995) 'Research roundup: research diaries and the research process', *Sociology Review* 4(3), February.

Edgell, S. (1980) *Middle-Class Couples*. London: Allen & Unwin.

Erikson, R. and Goldthorpe, J. (1993) *The Constant Flux*. Oxford: Clarendon Press.

Ferguson, M. (1983) *Forever Feminine: Women's Magazines and the Cult of Femininity*. London: Heinemann.

Festinger, L., Rieken, N. and Schachter, P. (1956) *When Prophecy Fails*. New York: Harper & Row.

Feyerabend, P. (1978) *Against Method: Outline of an Anarchistic Theory of Knowledge*. London: Verso.

Fielding, N. (1981) *The National Front*. London: Routledge & Kegan Paul.

Fielding, N. (2001) 'Ethnography', in N. Gilbert (ed.) *Researching Social Life*, 2nd edn. London: Sage.

Fielding, N. and Thomas, H. (2001) 'Qualitative interviewing', in N. Gilbert (ed.) *Researching Social Life*, 2nd edn. London: Sage.

Filmer, P. (1998) 'Analysing literary texts', in C. Seale (ed.) *Researching Society and Culture*. London: Sage.

Finch, J. (1984) '"It's great to have someone to talk to": the ethics and politics of interviewing women', in C. Bell and H. Roberts (eds) *Social Researching: Politics, Problems, Practice*. London: Routledge & Kegan Paul.

Finch, J. and Mason, J. (1993) *Negotiating Family Responsibilities*, London: Routledge.

Fine, G.A. and Sandstrom, K.L. (1988) *Knowing Children: Participant Observation With Minors*. Newbury Park, CA: Sage.

Finkel, S., Guerbock, T. and Borg. M. (1991) 'Race of interviewer effects in a pre-election poll: Virginia 1989', *Public Opinion Quarterly* 55: 313–30.

Fishman, P. (1990) 'Interaction: the work women do', in J. McCarl Neilson (ed.) *Feminist Research Methods: Exemplary Readings in the Social Sciences*. London: Westview.

Flanders, N.A. (1970) *Analysing Teaching Behaviour*. New York: Addison Wesley.

Fogelman, K. (ed.) (1983) *Growing Up in Great Britain: Papers from the National Child Development Study*. Basingstoke: Macmillan.

Foster, J. (1990) *Villians: Crime and Community in the Inner City*. London: Routledge.

Fox, K. (2004) *Watching the English: The Hidden Rules of English Behaviour*. London: Hodder & Stoughton.

Frankenberg, R. (1957) *Village on the Border*. London: Cohen & West.

Frankenberg, R. (1966) *Communities in Britain*. Harmondsworth: Penguin.

Gans, H.J. (1962) *The Urban Villagers*. New York: The Free Press.

Gans, H.J. (1967) *The Levittowners*. London: Allen Lane.

Garfinkel, H. (1967) *Studies in Ethnomethodology*. Englewood Cliffs, NJ: Prentice-Hall.

Gauntlett, D. (2002) *Media, Gender and Identity*. London: Routledge.

Ghuman, P.A. Singh (1999) *Asian Adolescents in the West*. Leicester: BPS Books.

Giddens, A. (1984) *The Constitution of Society: Outline of the Theory of Structuration*. Cambridge: Polity Press.

Giordano, P.C. (1995) 'The wider circle of friends in adolescence', *American Journal of Sociology* 101: 661–97.

Glasgow University Media Group (1976) *Bad News*. London: Routledge & Kegan Paul.

Glasgow University Media Group (1985) *War and Peace News*. Milton Keynes: Open University Press.

Goldman, A. (1988) *The Lives of John Lennon*. Chicago: Bantam Books.

Goldman, R. (1992) *Reading Ads Socially*. London: Routledge.

Goldthorpe, J.H., Lockwood, D., Bechhofer, F. and Platt, J. (1969) *The Affluent Worker in the Class Structure*. Cambridge: Cambridge University Press.

Goldthorpe, J.H. *et al.* (1980) *Social Mobility and Class Structure*. Oxford: Clarendon Press.

Gomm, R. (2004) *Social Research Methodology: A Critical Introduction*. Basingstoke: Palgrave Macmillan.

Gomm, R. and McNeill, P. (1982) *Handbook for Sociology Teachers*. London: Heinemann.

Gouldner, A.W. (1973) *For Sociology: Renewal and Critique in Sociology Today*. Harmondsworth: Penguin.

Gregson, N. and Lowe, M. (1994) *Servicing the Middle Classes: Class, Gender and Waged Domestic Labour in Contemporary Britain*. London: Routledge.

Halsey, A.H., Heath, A.F. and Ridge, J.M. (1980) *Origins and Destinations: Family, Class and Education in Modern Britain*. Oxford: Clarendon Press.

Haney, C., Banks, C., and Zimbardo, P. (1973) *A Study of Prisoners and Guards in a Simulated Prison*, reprinted in D. Potter, J. Anderson, J. Clarke *et al.* (1981) *Society and the Social Sciences: An Introduction*. London: Routledge & Kegan Paul/The Open University.

Hanmer, L. and Saunders, S. (1984) *Well-Founded Fear*. London: Heinemann.

Hargreaves, D. (1967) *Social Relations in a Secondary School*. London: Routledge & Kegan Paul.

Harré, R. (1993) *Social Being*, 2nd edn. Oxford: Blackwell.

Harris, M. (1984) 'The strange saga of the Video Bill', *New Society*, 26 April.

Heath, A., Jowell, T. and Curtice, J. (1985) *How Britain Votes*. Oxford: Pergamon.

Hey, V. (1997) *The Company She Keeps: An Ethnography of Girls' Friendship*. Buckingham: Open University Press.

Hitchcock, G. (1995) 'Writing lives – life history, oral history and the human documentary tradition', *Sociology Review* 1(2): 18–23.

Hobbs, D. (1988) *Doing the Business: Entrepreneurship, the Working Class and Detectives in the East End of London.* Oxford: Oxford University Press.

Hobbs, D. (1995) *Bad Business.* Oxford: Oxford University Press.

Hobbs, D. (2000) 'Researching serious crime', in R.D. King and E. Wincup (eds) *Doing Research on Crime and Justice.* Oxford: Oxford University Press.

Hobson, A. (1998) 'Which research interview?', *Sociology Review* 7(3): 17–20.

Holdaway, S. (1983) *Inside the British Police: A Force at Work.* Oxford: Basil Blackwell.

Holdaway, S. (2000) 'Racism: responding to the Stephen Lawrence case', *Sociology Review* 9(3).

Holden, A. (2002) *Jehovah's Witnesses: Portrait of a Contemporary Religious Movement.* London: Routledge.

Hood, R. (1992) *Race and Sentencing: A Case Study in the Crown Court.* Oxford: Clarendon Press.

Hough, M. and Mayhew, P. (1983) *The British Crime Survey: First Report.* London: HMSO.

Hough, M. and Mayhew, P. (1985) *Taking Account of Crime: Key Findings from the Second British Crime Survey.* London: HMSO.

Humphreys, L. (1970) *Tea Room Trade.* London: Duckworth.

Hutton, Lord (2004) *Report of the Inquiry into the Circumstances Surrounding the Death of Dr David Kelly.* London: HMSO.

Irvine, J., Miles, I. and Evans, J. (1979) *Demystifying Social Statistics.* London: Pluto Press.

Jackson, B. and Marsden, D. (1962) *Education and the Working Class.* London: Routledge.

Jesson, D., Gray, J. and Tranmer, M. (1992) *GCSE Performance in Nottinghamshire: Pupil and School Factors.* Nottingham: Nottingham County Council, Education Advisory and Inspection Service.

Jones, D. (1996) *Crime and Policing in the Twentieth Century.* Cardiff: University of Wales Press.

Jones, T., Maclean, B. and Young, J. (1986) *The Islington Crime Survey.* Aldershot: Gower.

Jowell, R., Witherspoon, S. and Brook, L. (1985–99) *British Social Attitudes.* Aldershot: SCPR/Gower.

Kaplan, A. (1964) *The Conduct of Inquiry: Methodology for Behavioral Science*. San Francisco: Chandler.

Kinsey, R. (1985) *Merseyside Crime and Policing Survey: Final Report*. Liverpool: Liverpool Police Committee Support Unit.

Kuhn, T.S. (1970) *The Structure of Scientific Revolutions*. Chicago: University of Chicago Press.

Lacey, C. (1970) *Hightown Grammar*. Manchester: Manchester University Press.

Langley, P. (1999) 'The Registrar-General's scale is dead: long live occupational scales', *S Magazine* 2: 36.

Lane, T. and Roberts, K. (1971) *Strike at Pilkingtons*. London: Collins.

Laslett, P. (1977) *Family Life and Illicit Love in Earlier Generations*. Cambridge: Cambridge University Press.

Lawson, T. (1993) *Sociology for A-Level: A Skills-Based Approach*. London: Collins Educational.

Lawton, J. (2002) 'Gaining and maintaining consent: ethical concerns raised in a study of dying patients', *Qualitative Health Research* 11(5): 693–705.

Lee, R. M. (2000) *Unobtrusive Methods in Social Research*. Buckingham: Open University Press.

Lewis, O. (1964) *The Children of Sanchez*. New York: Random House.

Lewis, O. (1968) *La Vida*. London: Panther.

Ley, D. and Cybriwsky, R. (1974) 'The spatial ecology of stripped cars', *Environment and Behavior* 6: 53–68.

Liebow, E. (1967) *Tally's Corner*. London: Routledge & Kegan Paul.

Loader, I., Girling, E. and Sparks, R. (1998) 'Narratives of decline: youth dis/order and community in an English "Middletown"', *British Journal of Criminology* 38: 388–403.

Lobban, G. (1974) 'Data report on British reading schemes', *Times Educational Supplement*, March.

Lutz, C.A. and Collins, J. (1993) *Reading the National Geographic*. Chicago: University of Chicago Press.

Lynd, R.S. and Lynd, H.M. (1929) *Middletown: A Study in Contemporary American Culture*. New York: Harcourt Brace.

Lynd, R.S. and Lynd, H.M. (1937) *Middletown in Transition*. New York: Harcourt Brace.

Mac an Ghaill, M. (1994) *The Making of Men: Masculinities, Sexualities and Schooling*. Buckingham: Open University Press.

McDonald, K. (2001) 'Social documents', in N. Gilbert, *Researching Social Life*, 2nd edn. London: Sage.

McKeganey, N. and Barnard, M. (1996) *Sex Work on the Streets: Prostitutes and their Clients*. Buckingham: Open University Press.

McNeill, P. and Townley, C. (1986) *Fundamentals of Sociology*. London: Hutchinson.

Mack, J. and Lansley, S. (1985) *Poor Britain*. London: Allen & Unwin.

Macpherson of Cluny, Sir W. (1999) *The Stephen Lawrence Inquiry: Report of an Inquiry by Sir William MacPherson of Cluny*. London: HMSO.

Madge, C. and Harrison, C. (1939) *Britain, by Mass Observation*. Harmondsworth: Penguin (reprinted 1988 by Cresset Library).

Maguire, M. and Bennett, T. (1982) *Burglary in a Dwelling: The Offence, The Offender and the Victim*. London: Heinemann.

Malinowski, B. (1967) *A Diary in the Strict Sense of the Term*. London: Routlege & Kegan Paul.

Mann, P. (1985) *Methods of Social Investigation*. Oxford: Blackwell.

Marmot, M. (1995) 'In sickness and in wealth: social causes of illness', *Medical Research Council News* 65.

Mars, G. (1982) *Cheats at Work*. London: Allen & Unwin.

Marshall, G., Newby, H., Rose, D. and Vogler, C. (1988) *Social Class in Modern Britain*. London: Hutchinson.

Marvasti, A.B. (2004) *Qualitative Research in Sociology*. London: Sage.

Mass Observation (1987) *The Pub and the People*. London: Cresset Library.

May, T. (2001) *Social Research: Issues, Methods and Process*, 3rd edn. Buckingham: Open University Press.

Mayhew, P. and Mirlees-Black, C. (1993) *The 1992 British Crime Survey*. London: HMSO.

Mayhew, P., Elliott, D. and Dowds, L. (1989) *The 1988 British Crime Survey*. London: HMSO.

Milgram, S. (1965) 'Some conditions of obedience and disobedience to authority', *Human Relations* 18: 57–74.

Miller, R. L. (2000) *Researching Life Histories and Family Biographies*. London: Sage.

Mirlees-Black, C., Mayhew, P. and Percy, A. (1996) *The 1996 British Crime Survey: England and Wales*. London: HMSO.

Mirlees-Black, C., Budd, T., Partridge, S. and Mayhew, P. (1998) *The 1998 British Crime Survey: England and Wales*. London: HMSO.

Mirza, H. (1992) *Young, Female and Black*. London: Routledge.

Moores, M. (1998) 'Sociologists in white coats: experiments in sociology', *Sociology Review* 7(3): 2–4.

Moran-Ellis, J. and Fielding, N.G. (1996) 'A national survey of the investigation of child sexual abuse' , *British Journal of Social Work* 26: 337–56.

Morrison, D. (1994) 'From the Falklands to the Gulf – doing sociology and reporting war', *Sociology Review* 3(3): 21–4.

Morrison, D. (1999) *Defining Violence: The Search for Understanding.* Broadcasting Standards Institute/Institute of Communication Studies, Leeds: University of Leeds.

Newburn, T. and Hagell, A. (1995) 'Violence on screen: just child's play?', *Sociology Review* 4(3): 7–10.

Newby, H. (1977) *The Deferential Worker.* London: Allen Lane.

Oakley, A. (1979) *From Here to Maternity.* Harmondsworth: Penguin.

Oakley, A. (1993) 'Telling stories: auto/biography and the sociology of health and illness', *Sociology of Health and Illness* 15(3): 414–18.

O'Connell Davidson, J. and Layder, D. (1994) *Methods, Sex and Madness.* London: Routledge.

O'Donnell, I., Farmer, R. and Catalan, J. (1993) 'Suicide notes', *British Journal of Psychiatry* 163: 45–8.

Okely, J. (1983) *The Traveller-Gypsies.* Cambridge: Cambridge University Press.

Osborn, A.F., Butler, N.R. and Morris, A.C. (1984) *The Social Life of Britain's Five Year Olds.* London: Routledge & Kegan Paul.

Osborn, R. and Milbank. J. (1987) *The Effects of Early Education.* Oxford: Clarendon Press.

Owusu-Bempah, J. (1994) 'Race, self-identity and social work', *British Journal of Social Work* 24: 123–36.

Pahl, J.M. and Pahl, R.E. (1971) *Managers and their Wives.* London: Allen Lane.

Pahl, R.E. (1984) *Divisions of Labour.* Oxford: Basil Blackwell.

Parker, H.J. (1974) *View from the Boys.* Newton Abbot: David & Charles.

Patrick, J. (1973) *A Glasgow Gang Observed.* London: Eyre Methuen.

Pawson, R. (1999) 'Methodology', in S. Taylor (ed.) *Sociology: Issues and Debates.* London: Macmillan.

Pawson, R. (1995) 'Methods of content/documents/media analysis', in M. Haralambos (ed.) *Developments in Sociology*, vol. 11. Ormskirk: Causeway Press.

Pearce, F. (1990) *Second Islington Crime Survey: Commercial and Conventional Crime in Islington.* Middlesex Centre for Criminology, Middlesex Polytechnic.

Pearson, D. (1981) *Race, Class and Political Activism: A Study of West Indians in Britain.* Farnborough: Gower.

Pearson, G. (1983) *Hooligan.* Basingstoke: Macmillan.

Phizacklea, A. and Wolkowitz, C. (1995) *Homeworking Women: Gender, Racism and Class at Work.* London: Sage.

Philo, G. (2000) 'Media coverage of the developing workd: audience understanding and interest', www.gla.uk/departments/sociology/debate.html

Platt, J. (1981) 'Evidence and proof in documentary research', *Sociological Review* 29(1): 31–66.

Platt, J. (1993) 'Case studies: their uses and limits', *Sociology Review* 2(3).

Plant, M.A. (1975) *Drugtakers in an English Town.* London: Tavistock.

Plummer, K. (1983) *Documents of Life.* London: Allen & Unwin.

Polsky, N. (1967) *Hustlers, Beats and Others.* New York: Aldine.

Popper, K. (1934) *The Logic of Scientific Discovery.* London: Hutchinson.

Power, S., Edwards, T., Whitty, G. and Wigfall, V. (2003) *Education and the Middle Class.* Buckingham: Open University Press.

Pryce, K. (1979) *Endless Pressure.* Harmondsworth: Penguin.

Redhead, S. (1990) *The End-of-the Century Party: Youth and Pop Towards 2000.* Manchester: Manchester University Press.

Roberts, E. (1984) *A Woman's Place: An Oral History of Working Class Women 1890–1940.* Oxford: Basil Blackwell.

Roberts, H. (1981) *Doing Feminist Research.* London: Routledge & Kegan Paul.

Roberts, K., Cook, F.G., Clarke, S.C. and Semeonoff, E. (1977) *The Fragmentary Class Structure.* London: Heinemann.

Roberts, R. (1971) *The Classic Slum.* Manchester: Manchester University Press.

Robson, C. (2002) *Real World Research*, 2nd edn. Oxford: Blackwell.

Rose, G. (2001) *Visual Methodologies.* London: Sage.

Rose, S. (1998) *Lifelines.* Harmondsworth: Penguin.

Roseneil, S. (1995) *Disarming Patriarchy: Feminism and Political Action at Greenham.* Buckingham: Open University Press.

Rosenhan, D.L. (1973) 'On being sane in insane places', *Science* 179: 250–8.

Rosenthal, R. and Jacobson, L. (1968) *Pygmalion in the Classroom.* New York: Holt, Rinehart & Winston.

Rosnow, R.L. and Rosenthal, R. (1997) *People Studying People: Artifacts and Ethics in Behavioral Research.* New York: W.H. Freeman.

Sanders, W.B. (1976) *The Sociologist as Detective*. Westport: Praeger.

Saunders, P. (1990) *A Nation of Home Owners*. London: Unwin Hyman.

Sayer, A. (2000) *Realism and Social Science*. London: Sage.

Schegloff, E. (1988) 'Goffman and the analysis of conversation', in P. Drew and A. Wootton (eds) *Erving Goffman: Exploring the Interaction Order*. Cambridge: Polity Press.

Schofield, M. (1965) *The Sexual Behaviour of Young People*. Harlow: Longman.

Scott, J. (1990) *A Matter of Record*. Cambridge: Polity Press.

Sewell, A. (1997) *Black Masculinities and Schooling*. Stoke on Trent: Trentham Books.

Sharpe, K. (1998) *Red Light, Blue Light: Prostitutes, Punters and the Police*. Aldershot: Ashgate.

Sharpe, K. (2000) 'Sad, bad and (sometimes) dangerous to know: street corner research with prostitutes, punters and the police', in R.D. King and E. Wincup (eds) *Doing Research on Crime and Justice*. Oxford: Oxford University Press.

Silverman, D. (1997) *Qualitative Research: Theory, Method and Practice*. London: Sage.

Sklair, L. (1991) *Sociology of the Global System*. Brighton: Harvester Wheatsheaf.

Smith, D.J. (1977) *Racial Disadvantage in Britain: The PEP Report*. Harmondsworth: Penguin.

Smith, D.J. (1983) *Police and People in London*. London: Policy Studies Institute.

Smith, D. and Tomlinson, S. (1989) *The School Effect: A Study of Multi-Racial Comprehensives*. London: Policy Studies Institute.

Stacey, M. (1960) *Tradition and Change: A Study of Banbury*. Oxford: Oxford University Press.

Stacey, M. (1975) *Power, Persistence and Change: A Second Study of Banbury*. London: Routledge & Kegan Paul.

Stein, S. (2002) *Sociology on the Web*. Harlow: Prentice-Hall.

Suls, J. and Rostow, R. (1988) 'Artifacts in psychological experiments', in J. Marowski (ed.) *The Rise of Experimentation in American Psychology*. London: Yale University Press.

Taylor, L. (1984) *In the Underworld*. Oxford: Basil Blackwell.

Taylor, L. and Mullan, B. (1986) *Uninvited Guests: The Intimate Secrets of Television and Radio*. London: Chatto & Windus; London: Coronet, 1987.

Taylor, S. (1982) *Durkheim and the Study of Suicide*. Basingstoke: Macmillan.

Tedlock, B. (2000) 'Ethnography and ethnographic representation', in N. Denzin and Y. Lincoln (eds) *The Handbook of Qualitative Research*, 2nd edn. Thousand Oaks, CA: Sage.

Thomas, W.I. and Znaniecki, F. (1919) *The Polish Peasant in Europe and America*. Chicago: University of Chicago Press.

Thornton, S. (1995) *Club Cultures: Music, Media and Subcultural Capital*. Cambridge: Polity Press.

Townsend, P. (1957) *The Family Life of Old People*. London: Routledge & Kegan Paul; Harmondsworth: Pelican, 1963.

Townsend, P. (1979) *Poverty in the United Kingdom*. Harmondsworth: Pelican.

Townsend, P. and Davidson, N. (1982) *Inequalities in Health: The Black Report*, published as Part One of *Inequalities in Health*. Harmondsworth: Pelican.

Valentine, G. (1998) '"Sticks and stones may break my bones": a personal geography of harassment', *Antipode* 30: 305–32.

Van den Hoonaard, D.K. (1997) 'Identity foreclosure: women's experiences of widowhood as expressed in autobiographical accounts', *Ageing and Society* 17: 533–51.

Van Maanen, J. (1982) *Varieties of Qualitative Research*. London: Sage.

Wallis, R. (1976) *The Road to Total Freedom: A Sociological Analysis of Scientology*. London: Heinemann.

Webb, E.J., Campbell, D.T., Schwartz, R.D., and Sechrest, L. (1966) *Unobtrusive Measures: Nonreactive Research in the Social Sciences*. Chicago: Rand McNally.

Wellings, K., Field, J., Johnson, A. and Wadsworth, J. (1994) *Sexual Behaviour in Britain: The National Survey of Sexual Attitudes and Lifestyles*. Harmondsworth: Penguin.

White, N.R. (1998) 'The best years of your life: remembering childhood in autobiographical texts', *Children and Society* 12: 48–59.

Whitehead, M. (1988) *The Health Divide*, published as Part Two of *Inequalities in Health*. Harmondsworth: Pelican.

Whyte, W.F. (1955) *Street Corner Society*. Chicago: University of Chicago Press.

Wiliam, D. and Bartholomew, H. (2004) 'It's not which school but which set you're in that matters: the influence of ability grouping practices on student progress in mathematics', *British Educational Research Journal* 30(2): 79–93.

Williams, M. and Robson, K. (2003) 'Re-engineering focus group methodology for the online environment', in S. Sarina Chen and J. Hall (eds) *Online Social Research Methods, Issues and Ethics*. New York: Peter Lang.

Williams, T.M. (1989) *The Cocaine Kids: the Inside Story of a Teenage Drug Ring*. Reading, MA: Addison-Wesley.

Williams, T.M. (1992) *Crack House*. Reading, MA: Addison-Wesley.

Willis, P. (1977) *Learning to Labour*. Farnborough: Saxon House.

Willmott, P. (1966) *Adolescent Boys of East London*. London: Routledge.

Winlow, S. (2000) *Badfellas: Crime, Tradition and New Masculinities*. Oxford: Berg.

Wolf, D. (1991) *The Rebels: A Brotherhood of Outlaw Bikers*. Toronto: University of Toronto Press.

Woodward, K. and Watt, S. (2000) 'Science and society: knowledge in medicine', in D. Goldblatt (ed) *Knowledge and the Social Sciences: Theory, Method, Practice*. London: Routledge.

Worsley, P. (1977) *Introducing Sociology*. Harmondsworth: Penguin.

Young, J. (1971) *The Drugtakers*. London: Paladin.

Young, M. and Willmott, P. (1957) *Family and Kinship in East London*. London: Routledge & Kegan Paul.

Index